DONUT
NATION

A Cross-Country Guide to America's
Best Artisan Donut Shops

ELLEN BROWN

Books published by Running Press are available at special discounts for bulk purchases in the United States by corporations, institutions, and other organizations. For more information, please contact the Special Markets Department at the Perseus Books Group, 2300 Chestnut Street, Suite 200, Philadelphia, PA 19103, or call (800) 810-4145, ext. 5000, or e-mail special.markets@perseusbooks.com.

ISBN 978-0-7624-5525-6
Library of Congress Control Number: 2014948618

E-book ISBN 978-0-7624-5605-5

9   8   7   6   5   4   3   2   1
Digit on the right indicates the number of this printing

Design by Jason Kayser
Edited by Zachary Leibman
Food styling by Carrie Purcell
Prop styling by Mariellen Melker
Typography: Eveleth, Gotham, and Mercury

Running Press Book Publishers
2300 Chestnut Street
Philadelphia, PA 19103-4371

Visit us on the web!
www.offthemenublog.com

Dedication

As I look back on my career, the person
who was pivotal to the direction my life took
is Sheryl Bills Heckler, who hired me as
a cub reporter for *The Cincinnati Enquirer*
and then moved me to Washington to work
at *USA Today*. This book is dedicated to
Sheryl, with my lifelong thanks for the faith
she showed in my work and me.

CONTENTS

ACKNOWLEDGMENTS

While writing a book and developing recipes are solitary endeavors, transforming them into an exciting book to hold in your hands is always a group effort. My thanks go:

To Zachary Leibman of Running Press who edited this book and brought it to fruition, and to Kristen Green Wiewora, who launched the book and saw its value.

To Jason Kayser, the talented designer at Running Press who made these photos so dramatic and enticing, and whose design makes this book a delight to hold.

To Steve Legato, whose talent as a food photographer is only matched by his great taste in jazz.

To Carrie Purcell, the gifted food stylist who made all of these decadent delights for photography, and her assistant, Monica Pierini.

To Mariellen Melker, who once again provided the perfect props for each donut and its setting.

To Ed Claflin, my agent, for his constant support, encouragement, and humor.

To my dear family for their love and support, especially to Nancy and Walter Dubler; Ariela Dubler; Jesse Furman; Ilan, Mira, and Lev Dubler-Furman; Joshua Dubler; Lisa Cerami; Zahir and Charlie Cerami; David Krimm and Peter Bradley.

To the many members of my vintage grapevine of food professionals who tipped me off as to where to find the country's most delicious donuts, including Christine Chronis, David Leite, Roberta Klugman, Carol Haddix, Leslie Cooper, Tina Antolini, Debra Ponzek, Marilyn Harris, Karen Berman, Joan Nathan, and John Mariani.

To my many friends who nibbled donuts and provided moral support, including Constance Brown, Kenn Speiser, Fox Wetle, Richard Besdine, Vicki Veh, Joe Chazan, Kim Montour, Nick Brown, Karen Davidson, Bruce Tillinghast, Beth Kinder, Ralph Kinder, Sylvia Brown, Kathleen Hittner, and Barry Hittner.

And to Patches and Rufous, my wonderful feline companions, who kept me company from their perches in the office and endorsed all the cream fillings when permitted.

PREFACE

Donuts are the great American equalizer. They're blue collar, they're white collar, they're at gas stations, they're on restaurant menus. They're at home in the boardroom and they're at home at the bowling alley. They appeal to all ages and across genders.

You can enjoy donuts at any time of the day or night, and you're likely to find bakeries that will sell them to you at any hour. You can still find wonderful donuts for less than a dollar, and even the biggest cities' most upscale bakeries sell them for just a few dollars. Donuts have not gone the way of the five-dollar cup of coffee and fifteen-dollar glass of house wine. While they may be the Champagne of confections, they're still priced on a beer budget—and a domestic beer at that. None of those fancy microbrews.

There's almost endless variety in the flavors and forms of donuts. Some days you may want a hearty cake donut, sometimes called a "sinker," to dunk into your favorite cuppa. Other times you want one filled with jelly or custard, or maybe a pretty French cruller with ridges visible through the glaze. And while most donuts are round, shaped like rings or circles, you can get them braided, square, with or without holes, and as long rectangles. If you don't want to commit to a whole donut, you can always munch the holes; they, too, have a lot of variety.

The American donut predates the Revolutionary War, and almost all international cuisines contribute some sort of sweet, fried treat to our melting pot. In many parts of the world, the local version of the donut is still made in home kitchens. But in Western culture we've by and large outsourced our donut-making. In that regard, donuts are similar to fried chicken: though people still *eat* fried chicken, rarely do they actually fry it themselves.

During the last half of the twentieth century, both donuts and fried chicken suffered the fate of burgers, pizza, and a growing list of other casual fare massacred and mangled by fast food chains. The chains eclipsed the mom-and-pop donut shops, in the same way that the Golden Arches dwarfed the burgers at independent diners.

But the desire for handcrafted artisan donuts is growing by leaps and bounds. New shops featuring classic and modern donuts are opening in small towns and big cities, reawakening the country's love of quality donuts. Donuts—especially fresh ones straight from the fryer—are hot! And there's nothing like the anticipatory aroma when you walk into a donut shop that cooks the treats on site.

I've had a wonderful time researching and writing this book. It was a delight to find donuts flavored with fiery sriracha sauce, resembling a pineapple upside-down cake, dusted with Chinese five-spice powder, or stuffed with foie gras. I have interviewed donut makers who are well-known national pastry chefs and others who are self-taught.

There are some exciting and delicious donuts being made in this country today. Luckily for us, the small shops that make their donuts, fillings, and toppings from scratch every day never really disappeared, and they have been joined by a new wave of innovative donut makers experimenting with whimsical forms and flavors.

While many of the original mom-and-pop donut shops were backed by small loans from the family or the local bank, some of the new shops are turning to the public, via Kickstarter campaigns, to fulfill their small but essential capital needs.

In this book, you will travel from Maine to Maui, and you'll see that this truly is a donut nation. Some of the shops profiled are now serving their fourth generation of customers, and still take total pride in their product. And it's that pride and insistence on quality that unites that coterie with the new donut shops that have opened their doors in the second decade of this century.

While this book is primarily prose, it also contains more than thirty-six recipes. The shops gave some to me, and others I developed. They are scattered throughout the text, and all of them have been tested numerous times in my kitchen.

When I get excited about a food, I usually want to cook it myself, and now you can, too.

Of all the food fads of the last few decades, the one that I never understood was cupcakes. I realize that it was rarely—if ever—adulation of the cake itself; that was the incidental base for the elaborate decoration topping it, the ultimate Martha Stewart fantasy. Any cook could make a cupcake, but the frills and flourishes added the wow factor.

But let's face reality. Cupcakes are almost impossible to stow in a backpack or purse without committing "icing-cide." And they are a committed dessert or celebratory food relegated to regimented eating occasions. It is rare to bring a box of cupcakes to a staff meeting or to eat an afternoon cupcake for an energy boost. Cupcakes don't dunk. They stand up and proclaim themselves. They demand attention.

Donuts are accessible and delicious. They're homey and friendly. Why would anyone covet a cupcake when he or she could devour a donut?

Nineteenth-century French gourmet Jean Anthelme Brillat-Savarin wrote in his landmark 1825 book, *The Physiology of Taste: Or, Meditations on Transcendental Gastronomy*, that "the discovery of a new dish does more for the happiness of the human race than the discovery of a new star." I can just imagine how happy he'd be eating a crème brûlée or lemon meringue donut.

Here's to donuts!

Ellen Brown
Providence, Rhode Island

INTRODUCTION
HOW WE BECAME DONUT NATION

Bits of dough have been fried in fat for centuries, and these treats remain popular around the world. But the all-American donut developed from a form brought from Holland to what is now New York in the seventeenth century.

The Dutch called the confections *oliekoeken* ("oily cakes") and fried them in pig fat. The same fried treats were also called *oliebollen* ("oily balls"), because of the irregular round shape caused by dropping the dough off the end of a spoon into the hot fat.

The change to the name "doughnut," or "donut" in this century, could have happened in a few ways. One theory is that the centers of the cakes once contained nuts. Another theory is that it was a typo—early bakers meant to call them dough*knots,* because the dough was tied into a knot shape, but the intended name didn't stick in the public's mind.

Regardless of what you call them, there's no question that donuts were part and parcel of life in New Amsterdam. In his 1809 book, *A History of New York,* Washington Irving, writing under the nom de plume Diedrich Knickerbocker, described seventeenth-century afternoon parties in New Amsterdam:

"Sometimes the table was graced with immense apple pies, or saucers full of preserved peaches and pears; but it was always sure to boast an enormous dish of balls of sweetened dough, fried in hog's fat, and called doughnuts, or *olykoeks*—a delicious kind of cake, at present scarce known in this city, except in genuine Dutch families."

By the end of the Revolutionary War, donuts had left the world of ethnic Dutch cooking and had been accepted as truly American. The first printed donut recipe in an American cookbook dates from 1803, in Susannah Carter's *The Frugal Housewife*, and an almost identical recipe appeared in the 1805 edition of *The Art of Cookery Made Plain and Easy* by Mrs. Hannah Glasse. In both books the recipe appears in a section titled "Several New Receipts Adapted to the American Mode of Cooking."

Interestingly, while in most European countries donuts were associated with specific holidays, especially the Christmas season and just before the start of Lent, none of these early cookbooks made reference to them as a celebratory food. They were just part of the "American Mode of Cooking."

The American donut, either made in home kitchens or at small bakeries, continued fairly unchanged for more than a century. And then in 1920, about a decade after Ford introduced the Model T, Adolph Levitt, who had fled czarist Russia for New York a few decades before, invented a machine to automate the production of donuts.

Levitt's machine formed and plopped perfectly shaped rings of dough into a vat of boiling oil, turned them at the exact moment needed, and then pushed them out of the machine onto a waiting draining board. The machine, the first of which was located in Levitt's bakery in New York's Theater District, was soon placed in the front window so a passersby could watch the miraculous process from dough to donut, thus reinforcing the American love of the form.

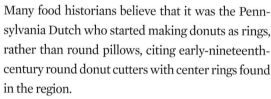

THE SAGA OF THE DONUT HOLE

Many food historians believe that it was the Pennsylvania Dutch who started making donuts as rings, rather than round pillows, citing early-nineteenth-century round donut cutters with center rings found in the region.

The hole became necessary to compensate for the addition of egg yolks to many donut recipes. Eggs and yolks created a sturdier finished product, but also made the dough denser, leading to raw donut centers. When ring shapes are fried, however, the heat of the oil penetrates from both the exterior of the ring and the rim of the hole into the dough, resulting in evenly cooked donuts. Donut cutters with a core attached were sold in the late-nineteenth-century Sears and Roebuck catalogs for an outrageous cost of four cents.

But let's not allow reality to get in the way of a good story.

Another version of the donut hole's origin, which has been transmitted for generations, is that a sailor born in Rockport, Maine, Captain Hanson Gregory, invented the donut hole in 1847. He hit rough seas and had to impale one of the donuts sent along by his loving mother on a spoke of the ship's wheel so he could use both hands for navigating.

When he went back to eating the donut, he found that the hole had dislodged all the uncooked dough, and he liked it so much better that way he told his mother about it.

In another version of the saga, Captain Gregory intuited that a round shape with a hole was the answer to the soggy donut center and fashioned a cutter for the hole from the top of a pepper tin.

While all of this is hearsay, we do know that John Blondell was granted the first patent for a donut cutter in 1872. It was made from wood and had a fluted edge. A version made from tin received a patent in 1889.

THE BATTLE BETWEEN DOUGHNUT AND DONUT

Certain shop owners, like Mark Isreal of Doughnut Plant in New York and Tres Shannon of Voodoo Doughnuts in Portland, Oregon, are adamant that the word is spelled D-O-U-G-H-N-U-T. Period. End of discussion. "You make doughnuts with *dough*, not *do*," Shannon says emphatically. When it's the name of a shop I've used their preferred spelling, although throughout this book I generically refer to the foodstuffs as "donuts."

There is no question that the longer name is the older one. The word "doughnut" appears in early-nineteenth-century cookbooks, although the idea of frying up bits of leftover bread dough dates back to long before the Romans.

But there is no consensus amongst food historians as when and how the shorter spelling entered the American vocabulary. John T. Edge, a Mississippi-based food historian and author of *Donuts: An American Passion* (G.P. Putnam's Sons, 2006), claims that the Doughnut Machine Corporation started it in the 1920s. Based in New York, the company wanted to sell its products in other countries and thought the phonetic spelling would be simpler.

Other histories have "donut" appearing in the 1880s, but all seem to agree that the spelling became popular when it was adopted by the Dunkin' Donuts chain in 1950. Following World War II, William Rosenberg started an industrial catering business with a few converted trucks around his native Worcester, Massachusetts, and he soon realized that more than 40 percent of the business was donuts and coffee. He launched the Open Kettle in 1948 in nearby Quincy, and the name became Kettle Donuts a year later. In 1950 he settled on Dunkin' Donuts, and five years later he sold his first franchise.

"Donut" is the preferred spelling in about half of U.S. publications. However, in Canada, Australia, and the United Kingdom, the preferred spelling remains "doughnut."

TALES OF DOUGHBOYS AND DOUGHNUT DAY

As Thanksgiving is mandated as the fourth Thursday in November, so Doughnut Day is pinned to the first Friday in June. While today the yearly food festival becomes a reason for product introductions by various chains and shops, the Salvation Army originally launched Doughnut Day in 1917 as a fund-raising event to support the war effort in Europe.

World War I, then called the Great War, was when Army soldiers became popularly known as "doughboys," and that moniker, too, involves the Salvation Army.

Soldiers were first called doughboys during the Mexican-American War in the mid-1840s. Marching in the Mexican countryside covered the soldiers with a coating of fine, white chalky dust, which made them resemble pieces of uncooked dough.

The connection between doughboys and donuts, however, dates to World War I in France. In 1917 the Salvation Army sent a small band of workers to France to help raise the morale of the homesick and frightened troops. The women were referred to as "Lassies" and they went into the trenches to hand out useful items and darn socks.

But the soldiers longed for foods from home, too. Making cakes and pies was out of the question because there were no ovens in which to bake them. But the Lassies could use some of the rations of flour and oil to fry donuts. They rolled the dough with wine bottles and cut out the donuts with whatever they could find. Some accounts say that the frying took place in metal helmets, but it's more likely to have been in larger vessels, like oil drums, especially since some reports talk about Lassies making more than two thousand donuts a day.

While the troops were being fed donuts, the Salvation Army was using the Lassies' work in France to raise money at home. Doughnut Day began as a high-priced bake sale. In New York, socialite Mrs. Vincent Astor allowed volunteers to use her kitchen overnight, an effort that netted more than 17,000 donuts for sale. Fund-raising via actual donuts gave way after the war to selling symbolic paper donuts.

But the most important contribution to the future of American donuts was when the doughboys came back at the end of the war. They waxed nostalgic and wanted more donuts.

While donuts are delicious, they are also big business in the United States today. On Doughnut Day in 2014, IBISWorld, a market research firm, published a report projecting that the donut stores industry will grow 2.4 percent annually, reaching $14.4 billion by 2019. The number of shops is anticipated to increase by 1.9 percent on average, to a total of 21,180, over the next five years. Dunkin' Donuts has announced plans for 400 new locations in 2014 alone. While much donut shop revenue comes from beverage sales and not donuts, that's still a lot of dough.

THE FAMILY TREE OF DONUTS

Key to the popularity of donuts are the many types of doughs, fillings, glazes, frostings, and toppings that can be combined in almost an infinite number of ways. A glaze made with fresh strawberries can easily top a strawberry cake donut, but it can also add color, shine, and flavor to the top of a yeast-raised round filled with homemade strawberry jam.

YEAST-RAISED

Yeast, the same living organism that makes bread rise, has been used for centuries to make donuts, too. In fact, bits of leftover bread dough were frequently fried up as a treat for the kitchen staff in wealthy American households in the nineteenth century. Yeast produces a light donut with a soft and airy interior. The basic glazed donut is typically a yeast-raised donut dipped into a vanilla or honey-flavored glaze.

Yeast dough formed into a pillow rather than a ring is the base for all the variations of jelly and cream-filled donuts. While the Boston cream donut has vanilla pastry cream inside and a chocolate glaze on top, pastry cream can be flavored with anything from key lime juice and lemon zest to chocolate or maple syrup. In some parts of the country, these filled donuts are called bismarcks, while in other parts they're bulls-eyes, and internationally these are *bomboloni* in Italy, *paczki* in Poland, and *sufganiyot* in Israel.

When the yeast dough is formed into a rectangle, it's called a bar, a stick, or a long john. And if the dough is braided in any way, it's a twist.

Two other regional forms of yeast-raised donut are malasadas and beignets. The malasada was originally Portuguese, and it was transported in the nineteenth century to Hawaii, where it's become the primary donut form. Malasadas are also found in mainland communities with Portuguese populations. The beignet is a French Creole variation, rolled thin and cut into squares or small rectangles for frying, and then heavily dusted with confectioners' sugar. It is found most often in Louisiana and on menus at Southern restaurants.

In 1963 President John F. Kennedy stood at the Berlin Wall and said "*Ich bin ein Berliner.*" It was a comment intended to show his solidarity with the people of that then-divided city; he was saying, "I am a Berliner." A Berliner, however, is also one of the names given to a jelly donut. In Berlin, though, the citizens call their jelly donuts *Pfannkuchen*, and no one thought the president had made a pastry faux pas.

CAKE

Cake donuts get their height from some combination of baking powder and baking soda, and it's a safe bet that any baked donut relies on these chemical leaveners. While I think frying is essential to a donut, baking them in special ring-shaped donut pans is a trend now on the rise.

In general, cake donuts are glazed or iced but not filled. The texture of the donut is dense and likely to crumble, and cake donuts almost always have a hole in the middle because the dense dough would be undercooked in the center otherwise.

Cake donuts' genealogy splits into two main branches. The first is a classic batter, thicker than a cake batter, that must be rolled. It can include anything from puréed fresh fruit, such as blueberries or peaches, to grated chocolate. Apple cider donuts, especially popular in New England in the fall, are a subset of cake donuts.

Old-fashioned donuts, sometimes called sour cream donuts or buttermilk donuts, have an irregular shape and get a crispier crust than other donuts. One reason is the formulation of the dough, and the other is that they are fried at a lower temperature for a longer period of time.

PÂTE À CHOUX

If you bake *pâte à choux*, it becomes big cream puffs or tiny profiteroles. When you fry it, you've got a French cruller or *zeppole*. In some parts of the country, crullers are called beignets, but they shouldn't be confused with New Orleans–style yeast beignets, like those served at Café du Monde (page 131).

In this classic French dough, the flour is cooked twice. The first time is in the pan, when the flour is added to boiling water in which butter has been melted, and the second time is in the heat of the oven or the fryer. What makes *pâte à choux* puff is heat and the power of eggs. The liquid in the dough creates steam in the hot oven or hot fat, and the gluten in the flour and protein in the eggs coagulate and create a hard structure around what is basically an air pocket.

A large star tip on the end of a pastry bag is what gives crullers their characteristic ridged shape. Traditionally they are just glazed after being fried, but a number of places now split them and fill them with custard too.

There are also savory versions of cream puffs. The most common is a small bite native to Burgundy called a *gougères* that's made with grated Gruyère cheese. I've discovered that they're even better fried than baked, so that's how I make them now. I've even made large ones to split and fill with creamed seafood as a dinner party entrée.

FRITTERS

Fritters are the ugly ducklings of the donut world, and that appearance is intentional. While other donuts are primped like a prom queen, fritters are unceremoniously plopped into hot fat. They can be made from either yeast dough or cake dough, and they can be either glazed or dusted with confectioners' sugar or granulated sugar.

Fritters are a delivery system for the food mixed into the dough. While that's most often chopped apples, peaches, or blueberries, it can also be sweet corn or sautéed onion.

HYBRIDS

Five years ago this section would not have existed. Then, in 2013, New York pastry chef Dominique Ansel, who chose to not participate in this book, "invented" the trademarked Cronut. A Cronut, and all of the variations on the same theme you'll find listed in this book under different names, is croissant dough cut into a round shape, fried, and then filled with pastry cream and given some sort of glaze or other top encrustation.

Croissants are made with what is termed "laminated dough," which alternates layers of pure butter with flour and water dough. It's laborious to make because the layers are created by a lengthy process of rolling and folding. Like phyllo dough, however, puff pastry or croissant dough is now available frozen in supermarkets, and few cooks make it by hand. The steam created when the water in the dough heats makes it rise and become flaky. As with *pâte à choux*, it's most often baked, but it can also be fried successfully.

But donuts have hybridized with other forms of breakfast and dessert too. Donuts and cannoli are joined at a few bakeries. At Frangelli's in Philadelphia, it's the cannoli filling of sweetened ricotta cheese that's inserted into a yeast donut, while at Psycho Donuts in California the filling is inside a donut, but then the whole donut is rolled in broken cannoli shells.

And finally there are two recent additions at Chicago eateries. There's the Wonut, created by owner Alex Hernandez at Waffles Café in Chicago. The thickened waffle batter is first cooked briefly in a waffle iron and then fried. And Enoch Simpson, the chef and owner of Endgrain, has merged donuts with biscuits to form the doughscuit.

MAKING DONUTS AT HOME

If you've ever rolled out piecrust, cut out sugar cookies, made a cream puff, baked a loaf of bread, or fried a French fry, you have the skills necessary to make any of the donut recipes in this book. Donuts are not rocket science or brain surgery. You make the dough, form the donuts, fry the shapes, and finish them with something as simple as a sprinkling of sugar.

Yeast donuts require more start-to-finish time than any other category of donut because the dough has to rise twice, and that can take a few hours. They're no more difficult than other varieties, but you do need patience and a warm spot for the rising.

I'm going to suggest adopting a thirty-year-old Dunkin' Donuts slogan for your kitchen: "Time to make the donuts!"

USEFUL EQUIPMENT

While some specialized equipment is needed to make donuts, none of it is expensive and most of it is probably already in your kitchen.

To make the dough, you need a mixer, measuring cups, and measuring spoons. For yeast dough, a stand mixer that can be fitted with a dough hook to knead the dough saves both time and energy.

To roll the dough, you need a rolling pin. But if you don't have one or it's busy propping open a window, you can use anything from a wine bottle to a cylindrical potato chip can. I like to roll dough on a silicone pastry cloth because I can load the messy, flour-covered cloth right into the dishwasher. You can equally well roll dough on a floured counter or cutting board, but then you'll have to clean the surface.

To cut the dough, you need some sort of round cutter. There are specialized donut cutters that come in a variety of sizes, or you can use any round object (and then a smaller round object to create the hole). If you want to make square donuts, you need a pizza wheel or just a serrated knife.

I am very fond of the stainless steel cutters made by Ateco. I have both the 3½-inch and the 2½-inch, and they are almost 2 inches high, which makes them easy to use. The company also offers a linked hexagonal cutter that cuts six at a time, which I use for filled forms such as jelly donuts.

I do not like the cutters from which the hole-cutter portion can be removed, because it tends to slip out when you want it in place. Round donuts without a hole can be cut with anything from a round cookie cutter to an overturned juice glass.

To fry donuts, you need a heavy-gauge Dutch oven or deep skillet that is at least five inches high. You'll pour two inches of oil into it, and it needs to be at least three inches higher than the level of the oil so that the oil doesn't splatter and catch fire. You'll be warned to not add too many donuts to the pan at one time, so it should be at least 10 inches in diameter—or you'll be frying donuts for hours.

To determine the temperature of the oil, you need a deep-fry/candy thermometer. This is one piece of equipment you may have to buy, but you really can't make donuts without it. Donuts are fried at very specific temperatures, and the oil should be kept at the correct temperature at all times. The only way to accomplish this relatively easy assignment is with a thermometer.

To finish the donuts, you need a wire cooling rack. The donuts go onto a rack set over a few layers of paper towels when they come out of the fryer, and, if glazed or iced, they go back onto the rack until the topping has hardened.

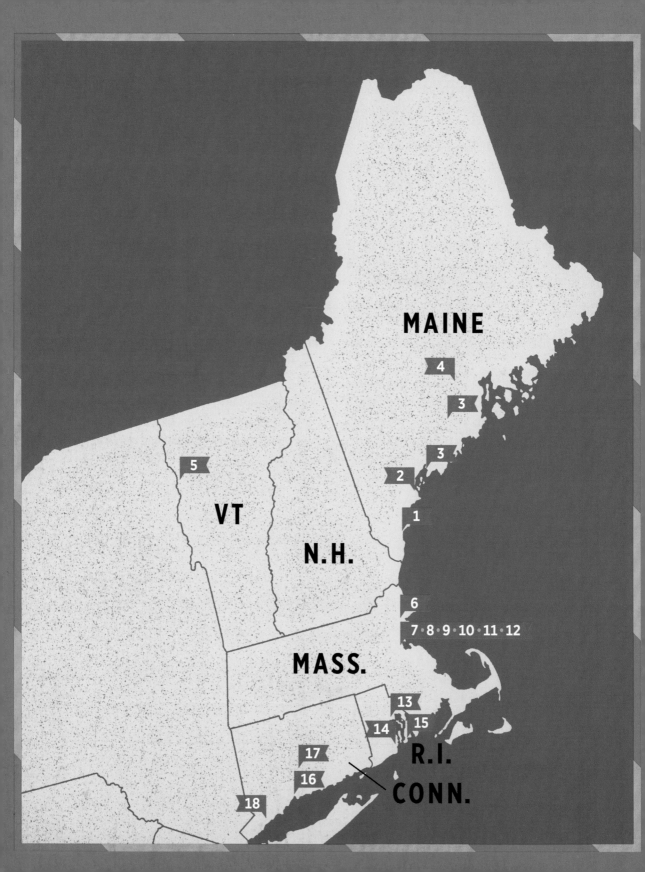

Chapter 1

THE NEW ENGLAND STATES

Perhaps it's because Dunkin' Donuts started in Massachusetts, but New England tends to boast more donut shops per capita than any other region. Another theory is that the Pilgrims, those folks who set up shop on Plymouth Rock in 1620, might have brought a recipe with them on the *Mayflower*. Most food historians credit the Dutch with the development of what we call the American donut, and the Pilgrims spent many years, after fleeing England, in Holland. So the theory is more than somewhat plausible.

Cake donuts, especially ones made with local apple cider, are very popular in New England. Maple flavoring is also a regional favorite, with or without bacon applied over the glaze.

CONGDON'S DOUGHNUTS:
FAMILY RESTAURANT & BAKERY

While there are extensive menus for both breakfast and lunch, and breakfast is served until the restaurant closes in the late afternoon, what put Congdon's on the map for natives and tourists alike is the donuts. The recipes remain the original ones formulated by founder Dot (Nana) Congdon in 1945, and while the business has been through some tough times in its seventy-year history, the donuts have remained its mainstay. And they're still fried in beef tallow the way Nana Congdon did it.

Clint and Dot Congdon moved from New Hampshire to Kennebunk, Maine, and opened a restaurant in 1945. The restaurant thrived, and a few years later they sold it and started a wholesale donut business out of their barn. The current location in Wells, about 100 miles north of Boston, opened in 1955. After a few fires necessitated considerable remodeling more than thirty years ago, the restaurant reached its present winterized configuration. A drive-thru was added in 2002 to ease congestion at the donut counter.

The business has remained in the extended Congdon family. Nana was in business with her son-in-law, Herb Brooks, first and now Brooks's nephew, Gary Leech, is at the helm.

People don't trek to Congdon's for donuts with whimsical names or newfangled combinations. They come for the cornucopia of old-fashioned cake and yeast-raised donuts that are fried fresh all day long; most customers report that the

Congdon's Doughnuts:
Family Restaurant & Bakery
1090 Post Road (U.S. Route 1)
Wells, Maine 04090
(207) 646-4219

www.congdons.com

donuts are still somewhat warm in the box. A large repertoire relies on either chocolate or vanilla cake as the base. These are topped with glazes ranging from maple to blueberry, and stuffed with Bavarian cream. The jelly donuts are filled with wild Maine blueberry jam, and local apples go into the apple fritters.

The yeast-raised donuts include the popular sugar twist and original honey-dipped; additionally, Congdon's makes a number of crullers, which are part of the New England tradition. "Our donuts are like going back to Grandma's house," says Gary. "It's all about nostalgia and comfort food."

Many first-time diners begin breakfast with a "Bowl of Holes," which is a way to sample the wide range of flavors. "It's like an appetizer at breakfast," says Gary. From this introduction, they decide which donuts they'll take home. They order them along with breakfast or lunch, and then pick them up on the way out.

The emphasis on quality donuts carries over to the savory food at Congdon's. The breakfast menu runs the gamut from simple eggs and pancakes to all manner of egg dishes, including eggs Florentine and Benedict.

Lunch features a range of burgers, sandwiches, and entrées with an emphasis on simple favorites, like New England baked beans or old-fashioned pot roast.

This is Maine, so lobster plays a role on the menu, too. There's a lobster roll at lunch, and lobster Benedict at breakfast. And if that isn't the ultimate Maine experience, there's one more. For $499 a group of six can accompany Gary to the docks one afternoon and select eighteen pounds of lobster to be transformed for them the next morning into the deluxe lobster Benedict—a half pound of lobster meat per plate under hollandaise with poached eggs. A dozen donuts are also part of the package.

VANILLA-GLAZED FRENCH CRULLERS

Makes 12

½ cup (1 stick) unsalted butter, sliced

1 tablespoon granulated sugar

Pinch of salt

¾ teaspoon pure vanilla extract, divided

1 cup all-purpose flour

4 large eggs, at room temperature

Vegetable oil for frying

2½ cups confectioners' sugar

3 tablespoons whole milk

REAL CRULLERS are made from the same dough as cream puffs; it's called *pâte a choux* in French. What makes them puff up is the sheer power of what eggs can do when heated, which is why soufflés rise too. Along with cake donuts and yeast-raised donuts, these are the true classic of American donuts, especially in New England.

Bring 1 cup of water to a boil in a saucepan with the butter, sugar, salt, and ½ teaspoon of the vanilla. Cook over medium heat, stirring occasionally. Take the pan off the heat and add the flour all at once, stirring with a wooden paddle or wide wooden spoon.

Place the pan over high heat and beat the mixture constantly for 2 to 3 minutes, or until it forms a mass that pulls away from the sides of the pan and begins to film the bottom of the pot.

Transfer the mixture to a food processor fitted with the steel blade or to a stand mixer fitted with the paddle attachment. Add the eggs, one at a time, beating well between each addition and scraping the sides of the work bowl between each addition. The mixture should look glossy and be totally smooth.

Line a sheet pan with 12 (4-inch) squares of parchment paper. Fill a pastry bag with the dough and, using a large star tip, pipe it into a 2½-inch ring on each square of parchment paper. Place the sheet pan in the freezer for 30 minutes to make the rings easier to handle.

Heat at least 2 inches of oil to a temperature of 350°F in a Dutch oven or deep skillet. Place a few layers of paper towels on a baking sheet and top it with a wire cooling rack.

(recipe continues)

Carefully slide a few donuts into the hot oil, being careful not to crowd the pan and making sure that the donuts do not touch each other. If desired, place them upside down into the oil while still on the parchment paper, and then, after 10 seconds of frying, carefully remove and discard the paper using tongs. Cook, flipping once, for 1½ to 2 minutes per side, or until puffed and golden.

Drain the donuts on the rack, blotting them gently with additional paper towels. Fry the remaining donuts in the same manner.

Combine the confectioners' sugar, milk, and remaining vanilla in a shallow mixing bowl. Whisk until smooth. Dip the warm donuts into the glaze and return them to the cooling rack. Let the donuts stand for 20 minutes, or until the glaze hardens. Serve as soon as possible.

VARIATION: **Substitute rum extract for the vanilla extract and substitute dark rum for the milk in the glaze.**

THE HOLY DONUT

While Idaho touts its potatoes as a national treasure, you'd better not repeat that boast to the Downeasters of Maine. That state is also proud of its potatoes, and its sweet potatoes, too. And local potatoes are the "secret ingredient" to the success of the two donut shops owned by Leigh Kellis and her father, Allen. She was almost finished with her education to become a Spanish teacher back in 2011 when she was lured by the dream of donuts like the proverbial siren song.

In the two years since the first shop opened in 2012, she's gone from making ten donuts a day to making more than a thousand donuts a week. Other than now buying local potatoes that have been pre-boiled to her specifications, everything at the Holy Donut is still done by hand—from rolling and frying the potato-laced cake donuts to squeezing the juices for the fruit glazes. In addition to her father, both her mother and sister now work for the business.

Leigh prides herself on the purity of her ingredients and maintains that "donuts can be wholesome and made with healthy ingredients and still be intensely pleasurable and delicious." Not only are the potatoes local, but so are all the dairy products used also. The flour is milled by King Arthur Flour in nearby Vermont, and the glaze colors come from fruit or vegetable dyes (a combination of pomegranate and beet juices, for example, makes pink glaze). No high-fructose

194 Park Avenue
Portland, Maine 04101
(207) 874-7774

7 Exchange Street
Portland, Maine 04101
(207) 775-7776

www.theholydonut.com

corn syrup or hydrogenated oils in this kitchen; Leigh's sweetener is cane sugar and the donuts are fried in pure canola oil.

In addition to the potato dough, Leigh makes both yeast-raised donuts and gluten-free donuts daily. In a short time the shop has developed a list of signature donuts. The most popular is a dark chocolate donut sprinkled with large crystals of sea salt, and a savory bacon- and cheddar-stuffed donut. Leigh uses high-quality imported cocoa powder and 60 percent cacao chocolate bars in all her chocolate products, some of which have accents ranging from ginger to cinnamon to coconut to vanilla.

Other donuts cycle onto the menu seasonally: the sweet potato ginger and maple-glazed donuts are popular in the fall and winter, while tart cherry and strawberry-glazed bring pastel flavors to spring and summer. And then there's the period in the summer when she can punctuate her donut dough with wild Maine blueberries, which appeals to locals and tourists alike.

But Leigh is always having fun experimenting. One of her latest concoctions joins her Maine potatoes with the state's prized crustacean, the lobster. While the dough is slightly sweet, so is the lobster meat, and Leigh fries a big chunk of it inside the dough, complementing the confection with fresh herbs. Perhaps you won't want to dunk this donut into your coffee, but then you wouldn't dunk a lobster roll either.

SWEET POTATO DONUTS

Makes 12

1 pound sweet potatoes

2½ teaspoons active
dry yeast

⅔ cup whole milk, heated
to 110°F to 115°F

¾ cup firmly packed light
brown sugar, divided

1 large egg

2 large egg yolks

4 tablespoons (½ stick)
unsalted butter, melted and
cooled

½ teaspoon salt

½ teaspoon ground ginger

3½ cups bread flour,
plus more for dusting

1 cup granulated sugar

1 teaspoon ground cinnamon

Vegetable oil for frying

IN ADDITION TO using Maine's white potatoes as a key ingredient in her donuts, Leigh Kellis also makes donuts from locally grown sweet potatoes at the Holy Donut in Portland, Maine. The rich flavor is balanced by a bit of sharp ground ginger.

Prick the sweet potatoes and microwave them on High (100 percent power) for 6 to 8 minutes, or until very tender when pierced with the tip of a paring knife. When cool enough to handle, peel and mash the sweet potatoes until smooth; you should have 1 cup of sweet potato purée.

Combine the yeast, warm milk, and ¼ cup of the brown sugar in the bowl of a stand mixer fitted with the paddle attachment, and mix well. Set aside for about 10 minutes while the yeast proofs.

When the yeast looks frothy, add the mashed sweet potato, remaining brown sugar, egg, egg yolks, butter, salt, and ginger. Beat well, then add the flour, and beat at low speed until flour is incorporated to form a soft dough.

Place the dough hook on the mixer, and knead the dough at medium speed for 2 minutes. Raise the speed to high, and knead for an additional 3 to 4 minutes, or until the dough forms a soft ball and is springy. (If kneading by hand, this will take about 10 to 12 minutes.)

Lightly grease the inside of a large mixing bowl with softened butter or vegetable oil. Add the dough, turning it so it is lightly greased all over. Cover the bowl loosely with a sheet of oiled plastic wrap or a damp tea towel, and place it in a warm, draft-free spot. Allow the dough to rise for 1 to 2 hours, or until it has doubled in bulk.

Punch the dough down. Dust a surface and rolling pin with flour. Roll the dough to a thickness of ½ inch. Use a donut cutter dipped in flour to cut out as many donuts as possible; alternatively, use a 2½-inch cookie cutter and then cut out holes with a ½-inch cutter.

(recipe continues)

Transfer the donuts and holes carefully to a baking sheet sprinkled with flour. Reroll the scraps one time to a thickness of ½ inch and cut out more donuts and holes. Cover the baking sheet with a piece of oiled plastic wrap, and let rise in a warm place until doubled in bulk, about 45 minutes.

Heat at least 2 inches of oil to a temperature of 360°F in a Dutch oven or deep skillet. Place a few layers of paper towels on a baking sheet and top it with a wire cooling rack. Combine the granulated sugar and cinnamon in a shallow bowl, and set aside.

Carefully add a few donuts to the hot oil, being careful not to crowd the pan and making sure that the donuts do not touch each other. Cook for 1½ to 2 minutes per side, or until golden brown and puffed. Drain the donuts on the rack, blotting them gently with additional paper towels. Fry the remaining donuts in the same manner. Once the donuts are cool enough to handle, dip them in the bowl of cinnamon sugar to coat. Serve as soon as possible.

I love donut holes, but if you want more real donuts and no holes, just add the holes back into the dough you're going to reroll for a second round. But dough can really only be rolled twice, so get as many donuts as possible by rolling the sheet into an even circle.

FROSTY'S DONUTS

Tourists might think that Frosty's Donuts was named for the climate of its home state. But the name is that of the first owners: June and Bob Frosty opened the shop in Brunswick in 1965. June passed away in 2011, and soon after Bob closed the shop and then sold it to another married couple, Shelby St. Pierre and Nels Omdal. Both of them grew up in Brunswick and had fond memories of Frosty's, but neither of them knew how to make donuts.

They certainly caught on quickly. In just three years, Frosty's has grown from a single shop in Brunswick to a mini-chain of four shops, and there is also a wholesale division that supplies Hannaford supermarkets in the state with donuts daily.

Shelby and Nels have kept many of the donuts invented by June and Bob Frost, including the chocolate coconut and a chocolate glazed. And many of the donuts are made with potato flour, always a hit in the nation's second-largest potato-producing state. Frosty's is particularly well

54 Maine Street
Brunswick, Maine 04011
(207) 729-4258

45 Main Street
Freeport, Maine 04032
(207) 865-9811

740 Broadway
South Portland, Maine 04106
(207) 699-4444

333 Water Street
Gardiner, Maine 04345
(207) 582-4258

known for a yeast-raised twist made with potato dough.

In addition to having added now-popular flavors like maple bacon to the roster, Shelby and Nels also introduced a DIY donut bar at the shops. Children and adults can select a donut base and then top it with anything from crushed Oreo cookies to gummy bears.

KENNEBEC CAFÉ

Central Maine doesn't have the cachet of the villages on the coast, but the small hamlet of Fairfield, with a population of around six thousand, might be where to find some of the most imaginative cake donuts in the country. Every day Ann Maglaras, who owns the diner with her husband, John, arrives a few hours before the open sign gets lit at 6:00 a.m. to start donut production. Ann is the "donut diva" until the restaurant closes at noon each day.

There's nothing fancy about the café. The painted sign on the drab gray storefront has the word "Pepsi" larger than the name of the restaurant, and John's repairs to the modest vinyl booths are done with duct tape. Their daughter, Megan Maglaras-Stevenson, is in charge of the savory side of the kitchen, which is known for its eggs Benedict (and occasionally eggs Warsaw, done with kielbasa instead of ham) and a hash brown potato casserole made with cheese, the recipe for which is a carefully guarded secret.

That leaves Ann to stay by her fryer, producing some of the sixty flavor combinations listed on her

The Kennebec Café
166 Main Street
Fairfield, Maine 04937
(207) 453-4478

donut board in the dining room. The base batter is made with buttermilk; all chocolate donuts contain real bittersweet chocolate; and the chai donuts are made after she has personally steeped a rich batch of tea.

While some of the options are fairly tame, including a basic old-fashioned donut and an aromatic sweet potato option, there are also ones like Olive Oyl at the Beach, tossed with a combination of salt, pepper, sugar, and olive oil. Others among Ann's favorites include the Jamaican Me Crazy, topped with bananas and cornflakes, and the Fatty Arbuckle, which is a whoopie pie donut topped with a peanut butter glaze.

But you have to enjoy them there. Ann can barely keep up with the donut orders from diners, so they do not sell them for takeout.

THE DOUGHNUT DILEMMA

SOUTH BURLINGTON, VERMONT

You can select a yeast-raised donut topped with a thick glaze of pure Vermont maple syrup, or you could have the same glaze on a banana cake donut. You could choose a jelly donut, in which the flavor of the homemade jelly changes seasonally. Or the same jelly mixed with natural, homemade peanut butter for a PB&J.

That's the dilemma confronting customers at the Doughnut Dilemma. So many decisions. Do you want a s'mores donut filled with homemade marshmallow fluff and topped with chocolate ganache and crumbled homemade graham crackers? Or perhaps you want a Funfetti, a vanilla cake donut with sprinkles in the dough and stuck to the top of the vanilla frosting.

The business, which opened in January 2014, is literally a cottage industry. It operates out of partner Michelle Cunningham's home kitchen. "I wasn't really much of a cook," says Michelle. "I thought the kitchen was a bonus room that came with the house." But all of that has changed.

"In Vermont it's very easy to be a licensed home bakery," says Michelle. That means that in Vermont, unlike in many localities, fledgling businesses don't have to operate out of communal "food incubator" kitchens like the one used by District Doughnut (page 97).

And while the legality is easy, the constraints of a home kitchen are daunting to her partner, Lauren Deitsch, a pastry chef trained at the Culinary Institute of America. Used to working in commercial kitchens, she now is limited to home equipment. All the donuts are fried in the same sort of electric fryer we home cooks use in our own kitchens; she just has three of them. And the Hobart mixer is of commercial size, but it could conceivably sit on the counter, which is why it's permissible.

On Tuesday, Wednesday, and Friday mornings the pair are up long before dawn to start their production for the day. Orders have to be placed by the evening before, and customers can either pick up their donuts at the house or, if they order a dozen or more, have them delivered. The women drop off donuts on the same days to a select group of wholesale accounts, ranging from the popular Cobblestone Deli to restaurants such as Bleu Northeast Seafood.

But their biggest venue is the Burlington Farmers' Market on Saturday mornings, where they will sell 600 to 700 of the 1,000 donuts they make each week. Friends may come by the market to help them by pouring coffee, and occasionally a friend joins them in prepping, but it's really just the two of them.

The Doughnut Dilemma
55 McIntosh Avenue
South Burlington, Vermont 05403
(802) 503-2771

www.thedoughnutdilemma.com

They are considering a brick-and-mortar shop with commercial equipment, but that would mean giving up their beloved farmers' market spot, according to the rules in Burlington. "The market is more than a place to sell donuts," says Lauren. "We've really bonded with other small food producers in the region." They will trade donuts for a farmer's fresh fruit to make a batch of jelly, too.

"Before we started the Doughnut Dilemma, Vermont had wonderful local butter and cheese, maple products, and great produce, but no donuts," says Michelle. But they've changed all that.

BANANA BREAD DONUTS WITH MAPLE ICING

Makes 18

DONUTS

3 or 4 very ripe bananas

4¼ cups all-purpose flour, plus more for dusting

3 tablespoons nonfat dry milk powder

2 tablespoons baking powder

1 teaspoon kosher salt

1 teaspoon ground cinnamon

1 teaspoon baking soda

3 tablespoons unsalted butter, at room temperature

⅔ cup granulated sugar

1 large egg, at room temperature

1 large egg yolk, at room temperature

1 teaspoon pure vanilla extract

1 tablespoon water

Vegetable oil for frying

GLAZE

1 cup pure maple syrup

4 cups confectioners' sugar

CAKE DONUTS flavored with puréed fresh fruit are a treat any time of year, and during Vermont's long winters, bananas are the fruit of choice. These donuts are topped with a glaze made from maple, the state's prized commodity. The second time I made these, I reduced ¼ cup of dark rum to 1 tablespoon, and substituted that for the water in the recipe.

For the donuts, purée the bananas in a food processor fitted with the steel blade or in a blender. Measure out 2 cups, and set aside. Combine the flour, milk powder, baking powder, salt, cinnamon, and baking soda in a large bowl, and whisk well.

Combine the butter and granulated sugar in the bowl of a stand mixer fitted with the paddle attachment. Beat at low speed to combine, and then increase the speed to high and beat until light and fluffy, scraping the sides of the bowl as necessary. Add the egg, egg yolk, and vanilla to the mixture and beat until fully incorporated. Add the banana purée and water to the bowl, and beat well.

Add the dry ingredients to the wet ingredients and beat at low speed until just incorporated. Scrape the dough onto a sheet of floured plastic wrap and pat it into a circle that is 1 inch thick. Refrigerate the dough for at least 2 hours, or up to 24 hours.

While the dough chills, make the glaze. Place the maple syrup in a shallow mixing bowl and slowly sift in the confectioners' sugar, whisking until smooth. Press a sheet of plastic wrap directly into the surface to keep it from hardening and set aside.

Heat at least 2 inches of oil to a temperature of 375°F in a Dutch oven or deep skillet. Place a few layers of paper towels on a baking sheet and top it with a wire cooling rack.

(recipe continues)

While the oil heats, dust a surface and rolling pin generously with flour. Roll the chilled dough to a thickness of $\frac{1}{2}$ inch. Use a $3\frac{1}{2}$-inch donut cutter dipped in flour to cut out as many donuts as possible; alternatively, use a $3\frac{1}{2}$-inch cookie cutter and then cut out holes with a 1-inch cutter. Transfer the donuts and holes carefully to a baking sheet sprinkled with flour. Reroll the scraps one time to a thickness of $\frac{1}{2}$ inch and cut out more donuts and holes.

Carefully slide a few donuts into the hot oil, being careful not to crowd the pan and making sure that the donuts do not touch each other. Once the donuts float to the top of the oil, fry them for 45 seconds to 1 minute per side, or until evenly browned.

Drain the donuts on the rack, blotting them gently with additional paper towels. Fry the remaining donuts and the donut holes in the same manner. While the donuts are still warm, dip the tops into the glaze, turning to coat them well. Place them with the glazed side up on a wire rack set over a sheet of waxed paper. Let the donuts stand for 20 minutes, or until the glaze hardens.

The donuts can be cut out and refrigerated for up to 1 day, lightly covered with plastic wrap. They should not be fried or glazed more than 6 hours prior to serving.

KANE'S DONUTS

The neighbors around Kane's Donuts in Saugus, a blue-collar enclave of about 26,000 located ten miles northeast of Boston, never need an alarm clock. Many of them naturally awaken every day around 3:00 a.m., because that's when they start smelling the donuts cooking in anticipation of the daily 3:30 a.m. shop opening.

Saugus, whose name comes from a Native American word believed to mean "great," was a country village when it was founded in 1629. It's now part of the urban sprawl of Boston, but it retains a sense of community, some of which is due to the three generations of residents who have made Kane's Donuts their breakfast spot.

Kane's was founded as a mom-and-pop donut shop by June and Bob Kane in 1955. Kay and Peter Delios bought it in 1988, and it's now run by their five children, who are teaching the next generation about the wonders of bismarcks, filled with blackberry jelly and whipped cream, and sour cream cake donuts. The latter are made in New England fashion, with spices like nutmeg, allspice, and cloves, and show the perfect amount of bubbling along the crispy edges.

In addition to a dedication to old-fashioned quality, Kane's also retains the feel of an old-fashioned, independent donut shop. It's the breakfast equivalent of the atmosphere popularized in the television series *Cheers*. All the regulars know one another's names, and the Delios family believes

Kane's Donuts
120 Lincoln Avenue
Saugus, Massachusetts 01906
(781) 233-8499

www.kanesdonuts.com

that "all customers should be treated like extended family."

The shop looks like a small New England cottage, and its interior has changed little in the more than a half century it's been in operation. There are a few tables with wrought-iron chairs and some stools at a counter in front of the windows. During the summer, there is also seating on a patio shaded by canvas umbrellas. Some of the original customers were in high chairs when they first visited, and now it's their grandchildren squealing with delight from their lofty perches.

The most popular donuts by far are the yeast-raised honey-dipped ones, which are suspended to dry by being threaded onto wooden dowels. Other traditional favorites are the Boston cream, honey-dipped filled with lemon curd, and red velvet. Certain donuts are seasonal, such as pumpkin and apple cider in the fall, eggnog in the winter, and pink lemonade in the summer.

While most donuts have been on the menu for decades, the five Delios siblings do keep adding flavor combinations. One of the more avant-garde is the crème brûlée donut, filled with pastry cream and then broiled to form a crispy caramel topping. Other recent additions are a caramel-frosted donut coated with buttercrunch, and a cake donut with peanut butter in the dough and filled with—of course—jelly.

The shop offers everything from breakfast sandwiches served on croissants to seasonal pies and strudels, but beyond the donuts there's just one real specialty. Peter Delios Sr. introduced a gigantic two-pound coffee bun that can easily feed a family of six.

"We come from a Greek background and part of that tradition is sharing food at the table," says son Paul Delios. "It's hard to share a single donut, so my dad came up with this idea."

APPLE CIDER DONUTS

Makes 18

2 McIntosh apples

2½ cups fresh apple cider, divided

3½ cups all-purpose flour, plus more for dusting

4 teaspoons baking powder

¼ teaspoon baking soda

2½ teaspoons ground cinnamon, divided

¾ teaspoon salt

¼ teaspoon freshly grated nutmeg

1⅔ cups granulated sugar, divided

3 tablespoons unsalted butter, softened

1 large egg, at room temperature

1 large egg yolk, at room temperature

¼ cup buttermilk

1 teaspoon pure vanilla extract

1½ cups confectioners' sugar

Vegetable oil for frying

WHILE JOHNNY APPLESEED made it as far west as Indiana planting seedlings, donuts made with apples and cider are most popular in New England. At some shops, the warm donuts are served with a small cup of apple butter, carrying the tantalizing taste even further.

Core and coarsely chop the unpeeled apples, and combine them with 1½ cups of the cider in a medium saucepan. Bring to a boil and cook, covered, over medium heat for 8 minutes. Uncover the pan and continue cooking until the apples are tender and the cider is almost completely reduced, about 10 minutes. Purée the mixture with an immersion blender or in a food processor fitted with the steel blade until smooth. You should have 1 cup of purée. Boil the purée to reduce further, if necessary. Set aside to cool.

Combine the flour, baking powder, baking soda, 1½ teaspoons of the cinnamon, salt, and nutmeg in a medium bowl, and whisk well.

Beat ⅔ cup of the granulated sugar and the butter with an electric mixer until combined. Beat in the egg and egg yolk, and then gradually mix in the apple purée, scraping the bowl as necessary. Beat in half of the flour mixture, then the buttermilk and vanilla, and then the remaining flour mixture. Mix to make a sticky dough; do not overmix.

Scrape the dough onto a sheet of floured plastic wrap and pat it into a circle that is 1 inch thick. Refrigerate the dough for at least 2 hours, or up to 24 hours.

While the dough chills, make the glaze: Simmer the remaining 1 cup cider in a small saucepan over medium heat until reduced to ¼ cup. Whisk in the confectioners' sugar until the glaze is smooth and glossy, and set aside. Combine the remaining granulated sugar and remaining cinnamon in a shallow bowl.

(recipe continues)

Heat at least 2 inches of oil to a temperature of 350°F in a Dutch oven or deep skillet. Place a few layers of paper towels on a baking sheet and top it with a wire cooling rack.

While the oil heats, dust a surface and rolling pin with flour. Roll the chilled dough to a thickness of ½ inch. Use a donut cutter dipped in flour to cut out as many donuts as possible; alternatively, use a 2½-inch cookie cutter and then cut out holes with a ½-inch cutter. Transfer the donuts and holes carefully to a baking sheet sprinkled with flour. Reroll the scraps one time to a thickness of ½ inch and cut out more donuts and holes.

Carefully slide a few donuts into the hot oil, being careful not to crowd the pan and making sure that the donuts do not touch each other. Once the donuts float to the top of the oil, fry them for 1 to 1½ minutes per side, or until evenly browned.

Drain the donuts on the rack, blotting them gently with additional paper towels. Fry the remaining donuts and the donut holes in the same manner. While the donuts are still warm, dip the tops into the glaze, turning to coat them well. Place them with the glazed side up onto a wire rack set over a sheet of waxed paper and sprinkle them with the cinnamon sugar. Let the donuts stand for 20 minutes, or until the glaze is set.

The donuts can be cut out and refrigerated for up to 1 day, lightly covered with plastic wrap. They should not be fried or glazed more than 6 hours prior to serving.

UNION SQUARE DONUTS

In the same way that the hip and happening food scene in New York has been migrating to Brooklyn, Bostonians are bidding adieu to Back Bay and ciao to Cambridge. Somerville, a formerly dilapidated blue-collar enclave a few miles from the Boston border, is where the action is, and that's where you'll find Union Square Donuts.

Union Square Donuts started on Valentine's Day of 2013, sharing a kitchen space with a few other food operations and selling maple bacon, chocolate chipotle, and Boston cream donuts off a folding table. The business was the brainchild of Josh Danoff, a food entrepreneur, and his siblings, and Heather Schmidt, a pastry chef who worked for chef Jody Adams at Rialto in Cambridge and Clear Flour Bread, a famous bakery in nearby Brookline.

"Our parents had a natural food store in western Massachusetts, and our grandmother lived on the Upper East Side of Manhattan," Josh says. "The whole family just sat around various kitchen tables, ate, and talked about food."

It was Heather who is responsible for the tantalizing texture of the donuts made at Union Square. Her dough is a sweetened yeast dough, but it is much closer to a rich brioche bread dough than a standard donut dough. The donuts have a crisp exterior and a light interior that offers up a bit of resistance when you bite off a chunk—and there are a lot of bites in each donut. Heather and her crew make everything from hand, using copious amounts

Union Square Donuts
16 Bow Street
Somerville, Massachusetts 02143
(617) 209-2257

www.unionsquaredonuts.com

of Cabot butter, a New England standard of quality. The fillings, glazes, and jams are also made right in the kitchen.

At $3.00 or $3.50 per donut, the prices are high when compared to donuts from a chain, but customers praise the generous portions and the thick and flavorful encrustation of toppings. Ones that remain on the menu are the always-popular maple bacon, the chocolate marble, the brown-butter hazelnut crunch, and the toasted coconut. "Donuts are a blank canvas," says Josh, "and there's almost nothing that won't be delicious as a donut."

In addition to the sweet donuts, Heather also makes some with savory fillings and toppings. Bacon cheddar sage donuts have become a signature alternative, and it's now joined by spinach feta red onion.

News of the wonders coming from Union Square's fryers spread rapidly through the community. The shop won the category "Best Donut of 2013" in *Boston* magazine's competition. And while it moved into a space by itself a few months after it opened, Union Square Donuts is still only open from Thursday to Sunday, and the short number of hours always have the caveat "or until we run out." That can be within a few hours of opening, so go early. Smart customers order a day in advance and rely on Union Square Donut's delivery service. It's one way to ensure they'll have their strawberry or chocolate marble with striped feathered icing like on a Napoleon.

The owners also have a great sense of humor. They include "apologies" and "bribery" with "weddings," "birthdays," and "bar mitzvahs" on the list of special events for which they can provide donuts.

JAPONAISE BAKERY AND CAFÉ

Boston is known for hosting some of the country's most innovative fusion food, such as Ming Tsai's menu at Blue Ginger in Wellesley. The fusion of pastry elements from Asia and the West has been happening at Japonaise Bakery and Café since 1985. *Japonaise* is the French word for "Japanese," and in the Japanese tradition, the bakery practices great attention to detail and restraint in the use of sugar. Owner and pastry chef Hiroko Sakan prepares the menu, including a range of donuts. On the savory side is a curry donut filled with Japanese-style beef curry that the bakery will gladly heat for customers.

The most unusual of the sweet donuts is the "an donut" filled with sweet red bean paste, azuki. While the an donut is a sibling of the jelly donuts, the filling is more dense and plentiful than your typical jelly. There are also both vanilla and chocolate cake donuts and a twisted donut, but be adventurous and try the azuki. If it's summer, top off your donut fix with a Japanese ice cream flavor, green tea or red bean.

You can find these fusion donuts at both Japonaise Bakery and Café locations.

Porter Square
1815 Massachusetts Avenue
Cambridge, Massachusetts 02140
(617) 547-5531

1020 Beacon Street
Brookline, Massachusetts 02446
(617) 566-7730

www.japonaisebakery.com

OHLIN'S BAKERY

It's difficult to find a Boston driving route that doesn't pass at least two Dunkin' Donut shops per mile. That's why it's so encouraging that—even with high gas prices—people from all over the region trek to suburban Belmont for the donuts at Ohlin's. The bakery has been serving the community since the 1960s, and there are no bells and whistles; donuts are take-out only because there are no stools or tables.

But what Ohlin's does have is an amazing yet homey array of both yeast-raised and cake donuts, including a fall apple cider donut that has its own legion of fans. The donut size is generous, and customers rave about the texture. The cake donuts

Ohlin's Bakery
456 Common Street
Belmont, Massachusetts 02478
(617) 484-0274

have just the right crunch on the outside and softness on the inside, and the donuts are sometimes still warm as late as noon.

All agree that the apple fritter—if available—is one treat not to be missed. Inside its craggy exterior is a heaping amount of apples, walnuts, and raisins, wrapped in a cinnamon-scented dough. A thick layer of glaze on top brings it all together.

THE GALLOWS

There's a lot of frying going on at the Gallows, a sophisticated New American bistro in Boston's South End, so donuts were a natural addition to the menu. Owner Rebecca Roth Gullo became so enamored with donuts after visiting The Doughnut Vault in Chicago (page 157) that she knew these fried pillows should be on her menu always.

The Gallows opened in June 2010, and Rebecca spent weeks at the Boston Public Library to choose its name. "Back in colonial times Boston was actually a peninsula formed by the Charles, Mystic, and Chelsea Rivers," she says. "The narrow passage that connected it to the mainland was called Boston Neck, and that's where public hangings took place." There's a black raven—a symbol of death—on the restaurant's sign and others mounted on the beige barn wood walls, too, along with a Ouija board and other ominous decorations.

While the name and decor might suggest a foreboding atmosphere, the popular Saturday and Sunday brunch in front of the huge picture windows is anything but. Like all the offerings at the Gallows, the brunch menu changes on an almost weekly basis, but certain favorite categories of food remain.

One menu standby is a breakfast donut sandwich, which is truly a savory treat, not just a sweet donut topped with some bacon. "It started out as a bacon, cheddar, and dill donut," Rebecca says of the additions made to the dough. But the donut became a true sandwich when it was sliced and filled with eggs and homemade sausage.

The Gallows
1395 Washington Street
Boston, Massachusetts 02118
(617) 425-0200

www.thegallowsboston.com

Blackbird Donuts
492 Tremont Street
Boston, Massachusetts 02116
(617) 425-0200

Donuts also feature prominently on the brunch à la carte menu. One week, the selection might be made with coconut milk, glazed with fresh mango, and then sprinkled with sweetened coconut; another time, it's yeast dough braided like a loaf of challah bread and served with dipping sauces including peanut butter mousse, strawberry tequila, and marshmallow fluff.

"We have a collaborative kitchen; all we do is think about food and then talk about it, and then come up with ideas for new donuts," says Rebecca. James Zilka, the sous chef in charge of brunch, makes the donuts. Zilka has experimented with his own donut/croissant hybrid, as well as with potato donuts and cake donuts.

The donuts share the fryer with other foods popular at the Gallows, which was selected in 2013 as the "Best Restaurant in the South End" by *Boston* magazine. There are always a few versions of poutine, the famous dish from Quebec province, on the menu; the hand-cut fries are topped with cheese curds made in the kitchen and a regularly rotating set of toppings—sometimes including sautéed foie gras.

One dish that's evolving with the Gallows' sausage recipes is the Scotch egg, which is served at all times of day. The eggs are soft-boiled, so even after being coated with sausage and panko breadcrumbs and deep-fried, the yolks remain soft.

Arancini, Italian fried balls of rice, are nontraditional at the Gallows, too. The Asian version is made with duck fried rice; fresh morels may be folded into the rice in early spring.

The Gallows is clearly in the camp of "farm-to-fork" cooking, so the menu changes often to take advantage of the bounty from local farms. Seth Morrison, the chef, looks to the bounty from the seas, too, and each evening's seafood entrées were swimming in local waters earlier in the day.

And now from Thursday to Sunday the donuts are easier to find because Rebecca opened Blackbird Donuts in January of 2015.

THE GALLOWS' SRIRACHA DONUT

Makes 18

2 (¼-ounce) packages active dry yeast

⅓ cup water, heated to 110°F to 115°F

⅓ cup whole milk, heated to 110°F to 115°F

5 cups all-purpose flour, divided, plus more for dusting

½ cup granulated sugar, divided

1 cup sriracha sauce

2 large eggs, at room temperature

6 tablespoons (¾ stick) unsalted butter, melted and cooled

Vegetable oil for frying

WHILE THIS RECIPE seems to call for a lot of sriracha, its heat dissipates into the donut, and you really need the large hit for it to lend its flavor and color to the donut. This is served at The Gallows as a brunch dish with fried eggs inside.

Combine the yeast, warm water, milk, and ½ cup flour in the bowl of a stand mixer fitted with the paddle attachment, and mix well. Set aside for about 10 minutes while the yeast proofs.

When the yeast looks frothy, add the sugar, sriracha, eggs, and butter. Beat at medium speed for 1 minute. Add the remaining flour, and beat at low speed until the flour is incorporated to form a soft dough.

Place the dough hook on the mixer, and knead the dough at medium speed for 2 minutes. Raise the speed to high, and knead for an additional 3 to 4 minutes, or until the dough forms a soft ball and is springy. (If kneading by hand, this will take about 10 to 12 minutes.)

Lightly grease the inside of a large mixing bowl with softened butter or vegetable oil. Add the dough, turning it so it is lightly greased all over. Cover the bowl loosely with a sheet of oiled plastic wrap or a damp tea towel, and place it in a warm, draft-free spot. Allow the dough to rise for 1 to 2 hours, or until it has doubled in bulk.

Line a baking sheet with parchment paper or a silicone baking mat sprinkled with flour. Punch down the dough, and transfer it to a well-floured board or counter. Roll the dough to a thickness of ½ inch with a floured rolling pin. Cut out 3-inch circles with a donut cutter dipped in flour, and transfer them to the prepared baking sheet. Reroll the scraps one time to a thickness of ½ inch and cut out additional rounds.

(recipe continues)

Cover the baking sheet with a sheet of oiled plastic wrap, and let rise in a warm place until doubled in bulk, about 30 minutes.

Heat at least 2 inches of oil to a temperature of 350°F in a Dutch oven or deep skillet. Place a few layers of paper towels on a baking sheet and top it with a wire cooling rack.

Carefully slide a few donuts into the hot oil, being careful not to crowd the pan and making sure that the donuts do not touch each other. Once the donuts float to the top of the oil, fry them for 1½ to 2 minutes. Gently flip them over with a mesh spoon or long chopstick and fry for an additional 1½ minutes, or until they are evenly browned.

Drain the donuts on the rack, blotting them gently with additional paper towels. Fry the remaining donuts in the same manner. Slice the donuts in half, fill them with fried eggs or the filling of your choice, and serve warm.

The donuts can be fried up to a few hours in advance. Reheat them in a preheated 150°F oven for 3 minutes, or until warm, before slicing and filling.

SOFRA BAKERY AND CAFÉ

★ CAMBRIDGE, MASSACHUSETTS ★

For donuts with the exotic lure of Middle Eastern flavors and spices, head to Sofra Bakery for weekend breakfast and relish the tahini brioche donut filled with brown butter cream and topped with salted caramel ganache. Pastry chef and co-owner Maura Kilpatrick, who worked alongside chef Ana Sortun at award-winning Oleana before the two collaborated on Sofra, adds sesame paste right into the brioche dough. Maura has been chosen four times as the city's best pastry chef by *Boston* magazine, and Sofra was selected as the city's best bakery when it opened in 2008. Other weekend options include donuts scented with Persian spices and a sour cream donut topped with chocolate "pearls." But the over-the-top creation is the one made with tahini, so get there early.

While you should always save room for the donut dessert, the food at Sofra also garners rave reviews. Groups frequently begin with selections

Sofra Bakery and Café
1 Belmont Street
Cambridge, Massachusetts 02138
(617) 661-3141

www.sofrabakery.com

of meze, including Moroccan-style carrot salad, stuffed grape leaves, and feta whipped with sweet and hot peppers. The breakfast offerings include *shakshuka,* poached eggs served in a tomato-curry broth, and *kuku,* a Persian-style herb omelet served with *labne* (yogurt cheese) and topped with buttery cracker crumbs.

While breakfast is served until 3:00 p.m. on weekends, heartier lunch options begin at 11:00 a.m. There are savory pies and stuffed flatbreads as well as *shawarmas,* which are stuffed with grilled meats.

FLOUR BAKERY + CAFÉ

In the fifteen years since she opened in Boston's South End, Joanne Chang has turned her empire of temptation into a string of four Flour Bakery + Café locations. On Sundays all of them make two very special donuts, one filled with homemade raspberry jam and the other filled with vanilla cream.

Joanne is an honors graduate of Harvard, and she was applying her majors in applied mathematics and economics as a consultant when she decided in 1993 to enter the professional kitchen instead. She was mentored by two of Boston's leading women chefs, Lydia Shire at Biba and Jody Adams at Rialto, before spending a year in New York at widely acclaimed Payard Patisserie and Bistro, and then returned to Boston and became pastry chef at Mistral.

The emphasis at Flour is clearly on the baked goods, both sweet and savory, and on taking homespun, old-fashioned ideas to a new level of sophistication. While such classic French forms as brioche and croissants are on the breakfast menu, so are sour cream coffee cake and sticky buns.

All of the hearty sandwiches are layered between slices of the bakery's exceptional bread, and they range from roasted lamb with tomato chutney and goat cheese to grilled Portobello mushroom topped with homemade pesto sauce. There is always a soup and a pizza of the day, and on the lighter side of the menu are some salads.

And the two donuts made each Sunday are worth an overnight trip to try.

131 Clarendon Street
Boston, Massachusetts 02116
(617) 437-7700

190 Massachusetts Avenue
Cambridge, Massachusetts 02139
(617) 225-2525

12 Farnsworth Street
Boston, Massachusetts 02210
(617) 338-4333

1595 Washington Street
Boston, Massachusetts 02118
(617) 267-4300

www.flourbakery.com

LA SALLE BAKERY

In the Middle Ages, St. Joseph, the patron saint of Sicily, saved the island from a terrible drought. Bakeries all over Southern Italy have been celebrating him every March 19 since with La Festa di San Giuseppe. The sweet finale to the feast is a crisp round of baked or fried dough topped with a crown of rich pastry cream and adorned with a candied cherry, called a *zeppola*. A *zeppola* is the Italian variation on the French cruller or the cream puff; it's formed from *pâté a choux* dough made on top of the stove rather than in a mixer. When I moved to Providence in 2003, I was told that Federal Hill was where I should go for all my Italian groceries, and that the shops along Atwells Avenue were the mecca for everything from fresh pastas to aged cheeses. But my foodie friends were quick to advise that "when you want the best *zeppole* [the plural form], you have to go to La Salle Bakery on Smith Street, beyond the State House; they don't get any better." Along with the traditional vanilla pastry cream version, La Salle Bakery also sells *zeppole* with chocolate or Bailey's Irish Cream liqueur in the cream topping.

And right they were! La Salle Bakery produces thousands of these traditional pastries each year in the small window of February 1 to the Saturday before Easter. Owners Cheryl and Michael Manni

993 Smith Street
Providence, Rhode Island 02908
(401) 831-9563

685 Admiral Street
Providence, Rhode Island 02908
(401) 228-0081

www.lasallebakery.net

have owned this fifty-year-old business for the past thirty-eight years, and their son, Michael Jr., is now the director of marketing and sales.

La Salle Bakery has won accolades from both professionals and loyal customers. In 2011 it was named "Retail Bakery of the Year" by *Modern Bakery* magazine, who chose from more than 24,000 bakeries. The next year it was chosen as the "Best Bakery in Providence" by the readers of *Rhode Island Monthly* magazine.

The bakery is also known for its wide range of meticulously decorated cakes, artisan loaves of crusty bread, European-style cookies, and all-American pies for the rest of the year. Christmas remains the busiest day of all. Both outlets also have breakfast pastries, including muffins and croissants, and serve savory food for both breakfast and lunch. But there's no single item on the extensive menu to rival the popularity of the *zeppole*.

ZEPPOLE

Makes 12

WHILE LA SALLE BAKERY knows there is a market for these Sicilian cream puff pastries all year, they only make them from February 1 to Easter, in honor of St. Joseph's Day on March 19. That's when Father's Day is celebrated in Sicily too. The thick, rich pastry cream tops the puff rather than fills it.

PASTRY CREAM

⅔ cup whole milk

1 large egg

2 large egg yolks

2 tablespoons cornstarch

3 tablespoons granulated sugar

1 teaspoon pure vanilla extract

ZEPPOLE

6 tablespoons (¾ stick) unsalted butter

½ teaspoon salt

2 tablespoons granulated sugar

⅛ teaspoon pure vanilla extract

1 cup all-purpose flour

5 large eggs, divided

12 candied cherries, for garnish

For the pastry cream, heat the milk in a saucepan over medium heat, bringing it just to a simmer, stirring occasionally.

Beat the egg, eggs yolks, cornstarch, and sugar in a mixing bowl with a whisk until thick and light yellow in color. Slowly beat about one third of the hot milk into the eggs so they are gradually warmed up, and then return the contents of the mixing bowl to the saucepan. Cook over medium heat, whisking constantly, until the pastry cream comes to a boil and thickens. Remove the pan from the stove and beat in the vanilla. Scrape the pastry cream into a container and press a sheet of plastic wrap directly onto the surface to prevent a skin from forming. Chill well before using.

For the *zeppole*, preheat the oven to 425°F and line two baking sheets with parchment paper or silicone baking mats.

Bring 1 cup of water to a boil in a saucepan over medium heat with the butter, salt, sugar, and vanilla, stirring occasionally. Turn off the heat and add the flour all at once, stirring with a wooden paddle or wide wooden spoon.

Then place the saucepan over high heat and beat the mixture constantly for 2 to 3 minutes, or until it forms a mass that pulls away from the sides of the pan and begins to film the bottom of the pot.

Transfer the mixture to a food processor fitted with the steel blade or to a stand mixer fitted with the paddle attachment. Add 4 of the eggs, 1 at a time, beating well between each addition and scraping the

(recipe continues)

sides of the work bowl between each addition. The mixture should look glossy and be totally smooth.

Use a pastry bag fitted with a large star tip to create circles 3 inches wide and 1 inch high, leaving 2½ inches between the puffs.

Beat the remaining egg with a pinch of salt, and brush only the tops of the puffs with a small pastry brush or rub them gently with a finger dipped in the egg wash. Be careful not to drip the egg wash onto the baking sheet or the egg will become glue that might keep the rings from puffing.

Bake the rings for 20 minutes, and then reduce the heat to 375°F and bake an additional 10 to 15 minutes. To determine if the puffs are done, look for even color on the top and bottom; they should sound hollow if tapped on the top.

Remove the rings from the oven, and using the tip of a paring knife, cut a slit in the side of each puff to allow steam to escape. Turn off the oven, and place the baked puffs back into the oven with the oven door ajar for 10 minutes to finish crisping them. Remove them from the oven and place them on a wire rack to cool completely.

To serve, place the chilled pastry cream in a pastry bag and pipe a crown of it on top of each pastry using a star tip. Then decorate the cream with a candied cherry. Serve immediately.

The puffs can be baked up to 2 days in advance and refrigerated, tightly covered with plastic wrap. Reheat them in a 350°F oven for 4 to 7 minutes, or until crisp. Then allow them to cool before piping the pastry cream on top.

The dough to make *zeppole* must be used warm, but it can be made up to two days in advance. Scrape it into a bowl, and rub the surface with softened butter to prevent a skin from forming. Reheat the dough over low heat, beating until it is just tepid to the touch, and then make and bake the *zeppole*.

ALLIE'S DONUTS

Everyone in the state touts Allie's Donuts in North Kingstown, home of the University of Rhode Island, as *the* place for donuts. This former sub shack on the side of the highway has been producing yeast-raised, cake, and old-fashioned options since 1968. But contrary to popular belief, Allie was not a woman. The shop was founded by Frederick Alvin "Allie" Briggs, and it is now owned by the Drescher family, who continue to import the flour from a small mill in Wisconsin.

Allie's is known for the size of its donuts as well as the quality. The average donut is huge by chain standards—and then there are the donut cakes for any sort of celebration. The cakes are made from yeast batter and can be shaped like an anchor—the state's official symbol—or any number for a birthday.

Allie's Donuts
3661 Quaker Lane
North Kingstown,
Rhode Island 02852
(401) 295-8036

MA'S DONUTS & MORE

The nineteenth-century whaling trade built a large Portuguese community in Rhode Island, so in addition to donuts you'll encounter authentic malasadas on occasion. The malasadas are part of the lure of Ma's Donuts & More, a shop that is open around the clock on Aquidneck Island. Valdemar and Palmira Leite opened the shop in 1993, and they create about forty-five types of donuts a day, ranging from hand-cut crullers to filled long johns and bismarcks. The coffee glaze is made with coffee syrup, a Rhode Island specialty. And, like at Allie's, the donuts are far larger than the current industry standard.

Ma's Donuts & More
78 West Main Road
Middletown, Rhode Island 02842
(401) 841-5750

But what's really special are the malasadas, especially when they come out from the kitchen warm. There's a drive-thru window, but don't be tempted unless it's the middle of a blizzard—you'll miss part of the experience if you don't walk inside and revel in the aroma.

ORANGESIDE DONUTS ON TEMPLE

Not only is necessity the mother of invention, in the case of the square donuts made by Tony Poleshek at Orangeside Donuts on Temple, the necessity became a trademark. "Home of the Square-Cut Donut" is the phrase emblazoned on the New Haven shop's website.

The shape of the donuts hardly limits the creativity with which they are filled, glazed, and encrusted with crunchy and soft toppings. The

Orangeside Donuts on Temple
25 Temple Street
New Haven, Connecticut 06510
(203) 773-1000

www.orangesideontemple.com

filled donuts are injected from all sides, so that there's not a single bite that doesn't include cream or jelly.

Tony had a background in donut-making. The native of East Haven, Connecticut, worked at a Mister Donut shop while attending high school and learned the tricks of the trade from master baker David Simoes. After a stint in the military, Tony began commuting to a desk job in New York City. But he and his wife, Michelle, decided that corporate life was not for them, and they opened a luncheonette in New Haven in 2009.

Workers at a nearby construction site requested donuts, and Tony couldn't find a vendor that produced the quality he thought his customers deserved. That's when Michelle suggested he start to make donuts himself. He invested in nearly $30,000 of equipment, but he refused to spend the next $100 for a round donut cutter. He cut the dough using a four-inch pastry cutter as a measure, and a two-inch square cutter for the hole.

Thus was born the square-cut donut. "I really think that rerolling scraps of dough after cutting round donuts leads to a tougher donut made from the scraps, and this way there are no scraps," says Tony.

The shop moved from Orange Street to nearby Temple Street in 2013 and became a full-service restaurant serving breakfast and lunch in addition to carry-out business. A year later, Tony and Michelle decided to sell the restaurant operation to Jacob Satir, and they began expanding their donut business beyond the few wholesale accounts they'd had for years.

Tony does both yeast-raised and cake donuts, and Michelle is still in charge of the decorating. "We've done over 150 combinations, and if a customer comes to me and challenges me to do the donut version of a non-donut dessert form, I'll do it," he says. One of the most successful experiments—now a shop signature—is the donut based on a Snickers candy bar: a chocolate cake donut is topped with a thick coating of chocolate, caramel, and peanuts. Another popular choice is the donut version of a Mounds bar, topped with dark chocolate and coconut.

Of the cake donuts, the blueberry—sometimes topped with blueberry glaze and other times with cream cheese frosting—and the chocolate are customer favorites. The lemon meringue donut is coated with meringue that is browned with a blowtorch, and another fruit pie derivative is the apple-filled donut.

What all these donuts have in common is the old-fashioned precision with which Tony crafts them. "They're all rolled by hand, cut by hand, and we don't use a belt fryer. We flip them one by one in the oil with a stick," he says.

NEIL'S DONUTS AND BAKE SHOP

Neil Bukowski, the owner of Neil's Donuts and Bake Shop in Wallingford, was a salesman back in the early 1990s. He didn't enjoy his job, and he longed to return to the era before box stores and chains ruled the world of baked goods. For a few years he worked his day job while apprenticing at night at a bakery to learn the tricks of the donut trade.

He opened the shop in 2001, and business has done nothing except grow. Summer used to be a slow season, but last summer Neil was selling out of donuts a few hours after his opening at 6:00 a.m.—so he started increasing production. "I never thought we would become a destination," says Neil, "but we now have people from all over the state coming and I don't want to disappoint them that we're out of donuts."

Each day more than thirty types of from-scratch donuts are fried fresh, starting from a range of handmade doughs. But Neil's is best known for its donut filling technique: be it key lime, lemon,

Neil's Donuts and Bake Shop
83 North Turnpike Road
Wallingford, Connecticut 06492
(203) 269-4255

www.neilsdonuts.com

Bavarian cream, Boston cream, or jelly, the donuts are split in half so a prodigious amount of filling can be inserted. "If you just fill from a hole in the side there are lots of bites that don't have filling, and this way they're even messier to eat but you really know you had a filled donut," Neil explains.

There's a whole line of cake donuts, including old-fashioned ones made with sour cream, plus French crullers glazed with various flavors of icing. And for customers who come early in the morning, Neil's also sells made-to-order breakfast sandwiches on fresh bagels. Neil believes that people wanting to escape from chain donuts also appreciate a breakfast that doesn't come in a plastic box.

COFFEE AN' DONUT SHOP

When most people think of the posh village of Westport, it's because of its famed former residents, who include Martha Stewart and Paul Newman. But donut devotees also know it for the Coffee An' Donut Shop, located behind a green awning on Main Street along with other mom-and-pop businesses. It's a spot where regulars sit at low stools at the counter and swap local lore with one another as they dip their donuts.

Coffee An' Donut Shop is owned by the Vlandis family, and has been open for more than thirty years. The full range of donut forms is made daily, and each has its avid fans. Customers queue up early to make sure they will be able to buy a chocolate cake donut or a coconut-glazed cruller.

The shop is also known for such creations as the marble twist, a braided combination of vanilla and chocolate yeast-raised doughs that is glazed after frying. The same vanilla dough is used for the honey glazed that are delivered on a stick from the kitchen in the back and nestled into the case.

But what amazes people is the texture of the cake donuts and how, when dunked into a cup of coffee, they better the flavor and texture of both. The exterior is crisp enough to withstand a dip, and the tender interior has enough heft that it doesn't disintegrate into the cup.

President Bill Clinton asserted that the donuts were the best in the country, and he had them shipped to the White House for Cabinet meetings. His picture is up on the wall, along with that of former Senator Joe Lieberman and an actor or two, including Robert Redford and Paul Newman.

Coffee An' Donut Shop
343 Main Street
Westport, Connecticut 06880
(203) 227-3808

NEW YORK

1·2·3·4·5·6·7·8·9

PENNSYLVANIA

13

10·11·12

N.J.

MD

DEL.

15·16·17

D.C.

14

Chapter 2
THE MID-ATLANTIC STATES

This is where it all began. The Dutch started frying up knots and then nuts of dough when Manhattan was New Amsterdam. A bit farther to the south, the Pennsylvania Dutch, in what was the nation's first breadbasket, became known for their fried treats like funnel cakes.

The Mid-Atlantic states love their donuts, and today's shops offer a wide range of both traditional and innovative forms. Manhattan and Brooklyn reign supreme among New York's boroughs for the number and quality of the donuts, and driving the I-95 corridor from New York to Washington is like a constellation of starring donuts.

Some of these shops have been in business for many decades, while others are brand new.

1. DOUGHNUT PLANT
2. DOUGHNUTTERY
3. DOUGH LOCO
4. SULLIVAN STREET BAKERY
5. BROOKLYN KOLACHE COMPANY
6. DOUGH
7. MIKE'S DONUTS & COFFEE
8. DUN-WELL DOUGHNUTS
9. PETER PAN DONUTS & PASTRY SHOP
10. BEILER'S DONUTS AND SALADS
11. FEDERAL DONUTS
12. FRANGELLI'S BAKERY
13. PEACE, LOVE & LITTLE DONUTS
14. FRACTURED PRUNE DOUGHNUTS
15. ASTRO DOUGHNUTS & FRIED CHICKEN
16. DISTRICT DOUGHNUT
17. FARMERS FISHERS BAKERS

DOUGHNUT PLANT

The legendary James Beard has been dubbed "The Father of American Cooking" for the influence he exerts to this day on food and chefs around the country. A subset of that title belongs to Mark Isreal, who started Doughnut Plant in the basement of a tenement on the Lower East Side of New York in 1994. He is clearly "The Father of the American Artisan Donut."

If imitation is truly the sincerest form of flattery, then no one should be more flattered than Mark. Countless donut shops around the country have copied his crème brûlée donut, which he started making in 2008; it's filled with custard and torched on top so the sugar becomes a crispy layer of caramel. He was also the first donut maker to use only fresh fruits in his glazes and to change them seasonally. When no one else had contemplated pistachio topping, you could find donuts with a thick green glaze and chunky nut pieces at Doughnut Plant.

The array of offerings at Doughnut Plant is staggering. There are not only yeast-raised and cake donuts, but also different shapes and sizes of each. Beginning in 2004, donuts no longer had to be just round: Mark began making them in squares so that they could be filled on all four sides with homemade jelly or custard. And while round donuts are certainly plentiful in the case, in 2012, smaller solid rounds—named Doughseeds—joined them. These mini donuts have innovative filling and glaze combinations: gianduja with chocolate

379 Grant Street
New York, New York 10002
(212) 505-3700

Hotel Chelsea
220 West 23rd Street
New York, New York 10011
(212) 505-3700

245 Flatbush Avenue
Brooklyn, New York 11217
(212) 505-3700

www.doughnutplant.com

glaze and chocolate hazelnut filling, blackberry filling with a coconut glaze.

While yeast-raised donuts were the mainstay of the business for the first decade, after five years of experimentation Mark started making cake donuts in 2008. Florence Fabricant, writing in the *New York Times,* called them "superb."

Two of Mark's most famous cake donuts are the Tres Leches, a donut version of the traditional Latin American cake, and the Blackout, which is a chocolate cake donut filled with chocolate pudding and glazed thickly with Valrhona chocolate to which chocolate cake crumbs are adhered. The Carrot Cake donut is filled with cream cheese-laced custard, and the donut itself is dotted with carrots, chopped toasted walnuts, and raisins.

By the time Mark started making donuts, the yeast-raised recipe had already been handed down through two generations of his family. Mark's grandfather, Herman, was an immigrant from Finland "who became a baker out of necessity," says Mark. He was stationed in Paris, where he worked as a baker, during World War I.

By 1931, when Mark's father, Marvin, was born, the family had moved to North Carolina, where his grandfather opened a bakery, making all his own products by hand. In the afternoon these included donuts, which Mark's father would glaze when he got out of school.

Mark moved to New York in 1981, and his first job was as a busboy at the famed disco Studio 54. The mirror ball in the bathroom at his shop in Chelsea is his homage to that time, and he recalls how "the [disco] interior was changed every night so customers never knew what to expect. That's what I want my shops to be also."

Although Mark was a toddler when his grandfather passed away, every customer who eats an eggless, yeast-raised donut can thank him. Mark was armed with his grandfather's recipe in 1994 when he began making donuts all night and then delivering them to shops on his bicycle all day. For the first few years, Mark's father worked with him in the basement bakery space. He would flip the donuts in the fryer as Mark cut them out.

While Mark's goal is to "keep coming up with donuts that are more and more delicious," he also wants his products to be healthier for customers than those made by his competitors. That's one of the reasons he sources ingredients locally and only uses them in season. Even the flour for his doughs is custom-milled to his specifications.

In 2000 Doughnut Plant got to move out of the basement and into its first shop on Grand Street. By then the donuts were well known and lines stretched out the door. The Chelsea location opened in 2011, and the Brooklyn outpost joined the ranks in the fall of 2014.

The decor of Doughnut Plant is truly donut chic. The walls behind the tables in the Chelsea shop are covered in stuffed donut-shaped and decorated pillows; they are artworks created by Mary Adams, a friend of Mark's. And Mark's father, Marvin, who is also a potter, made the donut tiles for all the shops.

The donuts are all handcrafted, so why the name Doughnut Plant? It's in memory of Mark's mother, who passed away in 1992. Every day, as his father was leaving for work, she would wish him well by saying "have a good day at the plant." And for the Isreal family, Doughnut Plant is the continuation of a family business into the new century.

In addition to the three shops, Doughnut Plant donuts are widely available at grocery stores such as Citarella and Dean & DeLuca, as well as at coffee shops and restaurants. Doughnut Plant donuts are even on the brunch menus of restaurants owned by famed chef Jean-Georges Vongerichten. There are also nine Doughnut Plant shops in Tokyo and one in Seoul.

DOUGHNUTTERY

A very large artistic component goes into creating innovative flavor combinations, but for the donuts at Doughnuttery, the artistry comes after the science. A robotic machine efficiently cooks the actual donuts at this stall in the popular Chelsea Market complex near the Hudson River. But then Evan Feldman's palate takes over, as the hot-from-the-fryer miniature donuts are coated with flavored sugars.

There are the classics like cinnamon sugar and confectioners' sugar. But then there are ones like The Cacaoboy, for which cocoa nubs are ground with chocolate cookies and mesquite-smoked sea salt, The Speckled Strawberry, which blends sugar with dried strawberries and the aromatic tanginess of lemon thyme, and the Purple Pig, whose purple color comes from the ground purple potato chips that are blended with maple sugar and ground bacon.

Evan became a donut devotee late in life, after a career in finance. His wife's family owned a bakery, and the extended family, regardless of their "real jobs" would pitch in and work there over the holidays. The foodie bug bit him, and when a space became available in Chelsea Market, he decided it was time to act on his donut fascination.

But the stall size is very small, so he and Katie Rosenhouse, a pastry chef who worked with him as a consultant to open Doughnuttery in December 2012, devised a plan.

Doughnuttery
Chelsea Market
425 West 15th Street
New York, New York 10011
(212) 633-4359

www.doughnuttery.com

The miniature donuts, which are only about two inches in diameter, are created from a dried mix formulated according to strict specifications. The batter is made in small batches by just adding water and kept in a hopper. When donuts are ordered, the machine pops them into the river of hot oil. Midway through the frying process—about 30 seconds later—the machine turns them over and then empties the hot donuts into a holding area.

"The machine could crank out 1,200 donuts an hour," says Evan, adding, "but we can only sugar and finish about half of that amount."

The topping combinations are made in advance, and not all are sweet. The PB&J is made from sugar mixed with ground peanuts and grape hard candy, but equally popular is the PBCP, a combination of peanut butter, cayenne, and pretzels. "I think of peanut butter as a blank canvas that can be transformed into many flavors," says Evan.

The donuts are sold in multiples of six. Two different flavors can be mixed in a half-dozen and up to four flavors in a dozen. Evan says that almost all customers select an innovative flavor for half their order and an old-fashioned flavor, like cinnamon sugar or vanilla sugar (made in house with vanilla beans placed into the sugar for two weeks), for the other half. "People tell me all the time that the old-fashioned ones remind them of their childhood," he says.

Evan uses pizza boxes for large orders of donuts, and he also caters everything from weddings to office parties, bringing a machine along to fry donuts on site.

While Doughnuttery does not fill its donuts, the shop does sell sauces into which the cake donuts can be dipped. Once again they combine tradition with innovation: Balancing the dulce de leche is a beer caramel sauce, and while the chocolate is deep and rich, there's some sparkle to the raspberry dip laced with heady balsamic vinegar.

DOUGH LOCO

New Yorkers believe that the division of the Upper East Side and East Harlem is around 96th Street, where the buried subway lines emerge from the ground beneath Park Avenue. It's there you'll find Dough Loco, the Lilliputian donut shop begun in 2013 by wunderkind Corey Cova.

He only makes one type of donut; it's a very high and fluffy yeast-raised puff stamped out with a five-sided roller. But what he then does with the flavor combinations in his thick glazes is truly magical. His richly toned blueberry glaze is made with a hint of aromatic rosemary, and then finished with lines of tart lime glaze randomly applied like an expressionist painting. Corey manages to turn browned butter into a material that can be sprinkled, and he uses it as the final encrustation on top of a pineapple glaze made from fresh pineapple that has been reduced.

Two of his most popular toppings incorporate Asian ingredients. Pure maple syrup is given a hit of umami with miso paste, and the bright red raspberry glaze has the fiery finish of sriracha sauce. The chocolate glaze is made from boutique

Dough Loco
1261 Park Avenue
New York, New York 10029
No phone at the shop

www.doughloco.com

Fruition Chocolate in the Catskill Mountains and has an almost coffee-like note in the finish.

Dough Loco makes only three or four donut options at a time, and the donuts frequently sell out early, so would-be customers sometimes have to wait up to an hour for the next batch. But that's less of an imposition when the new offering might include pumpkin topped with cherry or banana curry drizzled with dulce de leche.

Dough Loco is Corey's third venture into this neighborhood. The 2009 graduate of the Culinary Institute of America also created a menu of grilled cheese sandwiches for grown-ups at Earl's Beer & Cheese and a sophisticated snack menu for ABV Wine Bar. He raised the capital needed for refrigeration and other kitchen equipment at Dough Loco with a Kickstarter campaign for $7,000.

FLUFFY YEAST-RAISED DONUTS

Makes about 12

3 tablespoons bread flour

2½ cups all-purpose flour, divided, plus more for dusting

¼ cup granulated sugar

1 (¼-ounce) package active dry yeast

½ cup whole milk, heated to 110°F to 115°F

3 tablespoons unsalted butter, melted and cooled

1 large egg, beaten

½ teaspoon salt

Vegetable oil for frying

THE DONUTS at Dough Loco are much fluffier than the typical yeast-raised donut, and after a few tries, I think I replicated them well. The trick is called the Tangzhong method, and it involves cooking a small amount of water and bread flour to create a gel. When it's added to dough, it keeps the finished product moist and it also retards gluten development, making the donuts incredibly tender.

Whisk the bread flour and ½ cup water together in a small saucepan. Place the pan over medium heat and cook, whisking constantly, until the mixture thickens and swirl lines remain from the whisk. Remove the pan from the heat and allow the roux mixture to cool.

Combine ½ cup of the all-purpose flour, sugar, yeast, and milk in the bowl of a stand mixer fitted with the paddle attachment, and mix well. Set aside for about 10 minutes while the yeast proofs.

When the yeast looks frothy, add the cooled flour-and-water roux, butter, and egg. Beat well to combine. Add the remaining all-purpose flour and salt, and beat at low speed until the flour is incorporated to form a soft dough.

Place the dough hook on the mixer, and knead the dough at medium speed for 2 minutes. Raise the speed to high, and knead for an additional 5 to 7 minutes, or until the dough forms a soft ball and is springy. (If kneading by hand, this will take about 15 to 17 minutes.)

Lightly grease the inside of a large mixing bowl with softened butter or vegetable oil. Add the dough, turning it so it is lightly greased all over. Cover the bowl loosely with a sheet of oiled plastic wrap or a damp tea towel, and place it in a warm, draft-free spot. Allow the dough to rise for 1 to 2 hours, or until it has doubled in bulk.

Line a baking sheet with parchment paper or a silicone baking mat. Punch the dough down. Dust a surface and rolling pin with

(recipe continues)

flour. Roll the dough to a thickness of 1/2 inch. Use a donut cutter dipped in flour to cut out as many donuts as possible; alternatively, use a 3-inch cookie cutter and cut out holes with a 3/4-inch cutter. Reroll the scraps one time to a thickness of 1/2 inch and cut out more donuts and holes. Transfer donuts and holes to the baking sheet.

Cover the baking sheet with a sheet of oiled plastic wrap, and let donuts rise in a warm place until doubled in bulk, about 30 to 40 minutes.

Heat at least 2 inches of oil to a temperature of 375°F in a Dutch oven or deep skillet. Place a few layers of paper towels on a baking sheet and top it with a wire cooling rack.

Carefully slide a few donuts into the hot oil, being careful not to crowd the pan and making sure that the donuts do not touch each other. Once the donuts float to the top of the oil, fry them for 30 to 40 seconds. Gently flip them over using a wire mesh spoon or a chopstick, and fry for an additional 30 to 40 seconds, or until evenly browned.

Drain the donuts on the rack, blotting them gently with additional paper towels. Fry the remaining donuts and the donut holes in the same manner. Glaze the donuts as desired while they are still warm.

The cut-out donuts can be refrigerated for up to 4 hours. When ready to cook, allow them to complete their rising if they have not yet doubled in bulk. Fry them just prior to serving.

SULLIVAN STREET BAKERY

Almost all cuisines have a favorite form of fried dough, and in many parts of Italy it's *bomboloni*. The best *bombalone* to be found in New York isn't at one of the many ethnic bakeshops in Little Italy; it comes from Jim Lahey's shop in Hell's Kitchen, the Sullivan Street Bakery.

Jim has been dubbed the Bread Baron. He is now famous for his no-knead method of making bread, as well as for the quality of his signature *pane pugliese* and raisin walnut loaf packed with whole grains.

Bomboloni are the only sweet on the menu. The rounds are smaller than the average donut, so there's a built-in excuse for eating more than one. The pastry is rich with egg yolks and butter and is scented with lemon zest and vanilla. The classic filling is vanilla custard, although on occasion, chocolate custard is also on offer. Alternatively,

Sullivan Street Bakery
533 West 47th Street
New York, New York 10001
(212) 265-5580

www.sullivanstreetbakery.com

bomboloni are filled with seasonal fruit jam: strawberry rhubarb in the spring, raspberry or peach in the summer, and caramel apple in the fall and winter. Just before serving, they're lightly dusted with confectioners' sugar.

Jim returned from Italy, where he studied sculpture as well as bread baking, to New York in 1994. The shop is named for his first location in SoHo, and he moved to the present site in 2000. In addition to artisan breads, Sullivan Street is also known for its creative panini and pizza.

BROOKLYN KOLACHE COMPANY

You can take a girl out of Texas, but she'll always yearn for kolache (pronounced *koh-luh-chee*). At least that was true in the case of Autumn Stanford, who moved to New York in 2004 and really had a hankering for the Czech pastries she thought of as "road trip food" as a child. She ate them when traveling from her native Austin to visit her grandparents in Houston.

Eight years, a Kickstarter campaign, and many test batches of dough later, the Brooklyn Kolache Company opened in the spring of 2012 in the Bedford-Stuyvesant section of this up-and-coming borough. The menu offers a combination of sweet and savory kolaches, most of which are authentically Czech or authentically Tex-Czech—and then there are some combinations all Autumn's own.

"Kolaches are perfect for New Yorkers because they're portable, pre-made, and something new to discover," Autumn says. She makes everything except the peanut butter—used in combination with both jelly and chocolate—in the kitchen each day. She only makes one dough, which she describes as "slightly sweet and light, with a little chew and a yeasty finish." She uses the same dough for pigs-in-a-blanket, cinnamon rolls, and orange rolls.

On the sweet side, Autumn has a loyal Czech fan base scooping up such traditional fillings as poppy seed and prune, as well as her more Americanized combinations, like strawberry jam or blueberry jam joined with sweetened cream cheese. "People love these combinations in Danish,

Brooklyn Kolache Company
520 DeKalb Avenue
Brooklyn, New York 11205
(718) 398-1111

www.brooklynkolacheco.com

and in a kolache they get a larger fruit and cheese to dough ratio," Autumn says.

Some flavors of sweet kolache cycle on and off the dozen-a-day menu seasonally. Apple started out as a fall item but it is now permanently on the menu; peach and sweet cheese appear in the summer; and pumpkin custard kolache is for the winter.

The savory side of the menu is equally balanced between Texan favorites and Autumn's own innovations. The top seller is a combination of kielbasa, jalapeño slices, and American cheese, baked with a slice of hot pepper on top. "Some New Yorkers turn their noses up at American cheese, but that's the way they're made in Texas and the Texans who come in especially for them would be devastated if they were suddenly made with a fancy cheese," she reports.

Autumn makes the chili for her chili cheese dog kolache according to her mother's recipe, and she fills kolaches with smoked brisket in barbecue sauce or pimiento cheese—other famous Texas dishes. While the savory kolache sell well all day, there are more breakfast-themed ones made in the morning, vegetables with scrambled eggs or eggs, cheese, and hash browns. All the coffee is roasted down the block at Kitten Coffee, the first shop in New York to offer barista training classes.

Autumn had very definite ideas for the ambiance she wanted at Brooklyn Kolache Company. She had worked in cafes and bakeries before, and she instinctively envisioned an environment where customers would feel comfortable lingering. While free Wi-Fi was a given, she went much further with the help of her architect husband, Dennis Mendoza, who built some of the furniture, too.

Weather permitting, there's a huge garden at the back filled with climbing roses and grape vines that can be used for private events, too. The shop itself contains a piano, so musicians can entertain other customers, and a cache of board games is available for groups. The ceiling is high and huge windows allow light to pour in.

Autumn is expanding her base of Texans exponentially as word travels through the expat community. She even sells kolache as a pop-up some Saturdays at Skinny Dennis, a popular country bar in nearby Williamsburg. As her motto says: "Deep in the Heart of Brooklyn."

DOUGH

Dough's owner, Fany Gerson, believes that it's better to do one thing perfectly than to spread yourself out like an overly thin glaze. That's why this tiny shop in Bedford-Stuyvesant only makes large, yeast-raised donuts that are hand-cut and fried in small batches. No cake donuts, no old-fashioned donuts, and no crullers come out of the kitchen.

At any given time, there will only be two or three flavors, and there's no set schedule to determine what they will be when. But unusual combinations and vividly colored glazes always greet customers, and if you have time to wait a little, new flavors will emerge from behind the glass wall separating the kitchen from the tiny shop. The coffee is done in batches as small as the donuts; it's brewed in old-fashioned French presses as needed.

Dulce de leché topped with slivers of toasted almond has become somewhat of a signature item, as has lemon poppy, so those usually make an appearance at some point during the day. Another

Dough
305 Franklin Avenue
Brooklyn, New York 11238
(347) 533-7544

www.doughbrooklyn.com

year-round favorite at this shop, which opened in 2010, is the café au lait. It includes a sprinkling of freshly ground coffee beans and pecan praline chips on top of the milky glaze.

But then there are the truly innovative flavors. Fany was raised in Mexico and that heritage emerges with some combinations, such as the hot pink hibiscus glaze or passion fruit glaze sprinkled with cocoa nibs.

Dough's customers think they've won the lottery if there are jelly donuts—filled with one of Fany's legendary fruit preserves—available during a visit. Otherwise, they linger, hoping there will be soon.

MIKE'S DONUTS & COFFEE

This no-bells-or-whistles shop has been part of the landscape in Bay Ridge since 1976. While in this century, Brooklyn has become the spot where the chic come to consume everything from canapés to crullers, there are still blue-collar bastions feeding multiple generations of folks in their 'hoods. Mike's Donuts & Coffee is one of them.

Mike Neamonitis and his wife, Christina, are still working, and they've now brought their son Gus and son-in-law John into the business. The nondescript façade with red and blue letters and a "Donuts" sign extending out from the second-floor apartments is nestled between similar neighborhood spots.

An insistence on quality remains paramount to the operation. All the donuts, as well as muffins, bagels, bialys, and croissants, are made twice a day from scratch. And then there's the equal insistence on value. Mike's sells donuts for 75 cents each, or a dozen for six dollars, with an extra one for free. French crullers are one dollar, as are the "fancy" stuffed donuts.

The donut menu encompasses yeast-raised and cake as well as crullers, in flavors ranging from apple and cherry to all kinds of sprinkles—and even a whole-wheat donut. Mike's is what donut shops used to be about, and it remains a standard for other shops in the city.

Mike's Donuts & Coffee
6822 5th Avenue
Brooklyn, New York 11209
(718) 745-6980

www. mikesdonuts.com

DUN-WELL DOUGHNUTS

The owners hope customers will find the totally vegan options in this Williamsburg shop to be "dun-well," but the name is a combination of the last names of the owners, Dan Dunbar and Christopher Hollowell. The pair met while college students in Ithaca, New York, and, not finding an all-vegan bakery, they opened their own in 2011.

The donuts, almost all of which are yeast-raised, are made twice daily, and there are always at least a dozen flavors available from their list of more than two hundred. The menu reads like the one from every other donut shop: there are many like Boston "cream," raspberry "cheesecake," and cookies-and-"cream" that would traditionally be made with a dairy product, and then there are the

Dun-Well Doughnuts
222 Montrose Avenue
Brooklyn, New York 11206
(437) 294-0871

www.dunwelldoughnuts.com

vividly flavored fruity donuts like peach cobbler, raspberry coconut, and berry blast.

Signature flavors include the peanut butter and jelly, and The Elvis, which is peanut butter and banana. Candy bar–inspired flavors include the Almond Coco Joy and a faux Butterfinger. And while there is a maple donut, there's no bacon on it. Faux cheesecake is one thing, but faux bacon is another.

PETER PAN DONUTS & PASTRY SHOP

While Brooklyn is now home to hundreds of very trendy food outlets, one of the most popular has been in the same location for more than sixty years. Donna Siafakas and her family have run the Peter Pan Donuts & Pastry Shop since 1993, and they bought it from the original owner, who occupied the space for more than forty years.

The bakery is in the Greenpoint section of the borough, and that's where Donna's parents grew up and where they raised her. She went to St. Cecilia's Catholic School a few blocks away from the shop, and she says many of her classmates have come in for years—and now bring their grandchildren with them.

Peter Pan Donuts
& Pastry Shop
727 Manhattan Avenue
Brooklyn, New York 11222
(718) 389-3676

www.peterpan-donuts.com

"My husband learned how to make donuts while he was still in Greece, and that's all he's ever done," Donna says, adding that, back in the 1970s when there were many independent donut shops around, he would go from shop to shop each night as a freelance donut maker. In 1980 they opened their first donut shop, and then in 1993 moved to the Peter Pan space. The donuts are still made with all the original recipes they bought along with the physical space.

Donuts start going into the fryer at midnight, and they're made until late in the afternoon. "On a slow Monday we might just do one-hundred dozen, but on weekends or holidays we do three-hundred to four-hundred dozen a day," Donna says. Each donut is rolled, cut, fried, and topped by hand. The only machine in the kitchen is a cash register.

There are yeast-raised donuts, cake donuts, French crullers, and, around Lent, the traditional Polish donuts, *paczki,* are added to the mix in this predominantly Polish neighborhood. In addition to donuts, Peter Pan serves muffins, rolls, Danish pastries, and fruit turnovers. "It's an old kitchen and we all work together in close quarters, but we manage to make it work," says Donna.

While the recipes have remained the same, the popularity of certain donuts has grown in the decades the shop has been open. "It used to be about 85 percent yeast-raised donuts and now the percentage of cake donuts has grown from 15 percent to about 40 percent," Donna reports.

Some of that can be credited to the popularity of recent introductions, such as a red velvet donut and an old-fashioned sour cream donut with a simple glaze. During the summer, the red velvet cake donut can also be ordered split and filled with ice cream.

All of the donut fillings and glazes are made in the kitchen, and sometimes they borrow from another baked good tradition. There's a streusel topping on some donuts that also appears on the muffins, and Bavarian cream fills the layers of cakes as well as donuts.

Amid the crush of commuters stopping in for coffee and donuts to go, Peter Pan also serves eggs for breakfast, either on a bagel or roll or just on a plate. "We know our regulars and what they order every time they're in," says Donna.

OLD-FASHIONED SOUR CREAM DONUTS

Makes 12

3 tablespoons unsalted butter, at room temperature

½ cup granulated sugar

2 large egg yolks

¾ cup sour cream

½ teaspoon pure vanilla extract

1¾ teaspoons baking powder

¼ teaspoon salt

¼ teaspoon freshly grated nutmeg

¼ teaspoon ground cinnamon

2½ cups all-purpose flour, plus more for dusting

Vegetable oil for frying

OLD-FASHIONED DONUTS are a subset of cake donuts; they're fried at a lower temperature than most donuts and turned more often, so they emerge from the oil with lots of grooves and a crunchy exterior. They might not win a beauty contest, but their fans are totally loyal to them, and they take well to any manner of glaze.

Combine the butter and sugar in the bowl of a stand electric mixer fitted with the paddle attachment. Beat at low speed to combine, and then increase the speed to medium and beat for 1 minute, or until the mixture looks like coarse sand. Add the egg yolks and beat for 1 additional minute, scraping the sides of the bowl as necessary. Add the sour cream, vanilla, baking powder, salt, nutmeg, and cinnamon and beat well.

Add the flour and beat at low speed until thoroughly combined. Grease a large sheet of plastic wrap and scrape the dough into the center. Make the dough into a round pancake about 1 inch thick. Refrigerate the dough for at least 2 hours, or up to 24 hours.

Heat at least 2 inches of oil to a temperature of 325°F in a Dutch oven or deep skillet. Place a few layers of paper towels on a baking sheet and top it with a wire cooling rack.

While the oil heats, dust a surface and rolling pin with flour. Roll the chilled dough to a thickness of ½ inch. Use a donut cutter dipped in flour to cut out as many donuts as possible; alternatively use a 2½-inch cookie cutter and then cut out holes with a ½-inch cutter. Transfer the donuts and holes carefully to a baking sheet sprinkled with flour. Reroll the scraps one time to a thickness of ½ inch and cut out more donuts and holes.

Carefully slide a few donuts into the hot oil, being careful not to crowd the pan and making sure that the donuts do not touch each other. Once the donuts float to the top of the oil, fry them for 20 seconds.

Gently flip them over and fry for $1\frac{1}{2}$ minutes, then flip them again and fry for 1 to $1\frac{1}{4}$ minutes, or until evenly browned.

Drain the donuts on the rack, blotting them gently with additional paper towels. Fry the remaining donuts and the donut holes in the same manner. Glaze the donuts while they are still warm. Serve as soon as possible.

The donuts are best if eaten within a few hours of being fried, but they can be kept at room temperature, tightly covered with plastic wrap, for up to 1 day.

BEILER'S DONUTS AND SALADS

While visitors to Philadelphia flock to Independence Hall and the Liberty Bell, foodie tourists head to another landmark—Reading Terminal Market. Joining the ranks of culinary attractions in May 2013 was a stall with the unusual pairing of donuts with—wait for it—salads. At Beiler's Donuts and Salads, donut devotees can assuage their guilt and balance a sweet indulgence with a healthy option.

And sweet indulgences abound, filled as customers wait. The caramel apple donut is stuffed with a large serving of apple filling and topped with a thick layer of caramel icing. The filled strawberry donuts are rich with homemade jam.

Keith and Kevin Beiler run the donut operation, while their father, Alvin, remains at the helm of Beiler's Bakery in Reading Terminal. Beiler's Bakery was chosen by Fodor's travel guides as one of the top twenty dessert places in the country, and it has been a fixture in the community for more than thirty years.

The recipe for the yeast-raised donuts is a first cousin to the one from which sticky buns and cinnamon rolls are made at the bakery (other bakery favorites include whoopie pies and breads). The recipe's been in the family for generations.

The impetus for a donut shop really came from the customers. Every August, the market sponsors a Pennsylvania Dutch festival to celebrate that regional heritage, and for the festival,

Beiler's Donuts and Salads
Reading Terminal Market
12th and Arch Streets
Philadelphia, Pennsylvania 19107
(267) 318-7480

Beiler's Bakery would make funnel cakes and donuts. Customers clamored for the fried treats; there was no room in the space, however, to add donut production beyond for the special events. The spaces inside the historic structure are small and all of them are taken.

But the Beiler family also ran a shop called AJ Pickle Patch across from the bakery, selling packages and jars of Pennsylvania Dutch items along with fresh salads. The jams and jellies got pushed to the side, and donut production began in May 2013. By the end of that year, *Philadelphia* magazine had awarded them the title "Best Donut."

On any given day, about forty types of donuts are made on site, and all are filled to order. Gallon batches of custard wait to fill a Boston cream donut—before the top receives its traditional chocolate frosting—and large vats of cooked apples are ready for the harvest apple and caramel donuts.

In addition to the yeast-raised donuts, the shop also makes cake donuts and fritters that are dotted all the way through with fresh fruit. The list of options is varied and extensive, but not weird. There are no donuts infused with herbs or iced to resemble the Liberty Bell.

There are some modern touches. A cake donut iced with chocolate frosting has nuggets of brightly colored Fruity Pebbles cereal on top, and the Oreo-inspired donut is filled with a lighter version of the white cream sandwiching the cookies together, and then has crushed cookies on top of the white glaze.

But do plan a visit to Beiler's Donuts in advance. The shop is only open from Tuesdays to Saturdays because, in keeping with the family's Amish background, there is no work done on the Sabbath, and then Monday is just a day off.

READING TERMINAL MARKET

While the former train shed upstairs is now part of the Philadelphia Convention Center, the bustling market at street level is as busy as it was when it opened in 1893. Three of the current vendors are descendants of the building's original tenants.

The stalls are laid out in a grid pattern, with twelve narrow aisles running east to west, and four wider aisles dividing the space from north to south. A state-of-the-art (for the nineteenth century) refrigeration system installed in the basement allowed merchants to keep seasonal products available for much of the year. Whatever space remained after the merchants claimed their portions was leased out to restaurants for prepared food, to hospitals to store perishable medicine, and to local breweries for their hops.

Reading Terminal Market also set standards for customer service. Delivery boys called "market brats" delivered to in-town customers, and suburban shoppers called in their orders and had them delivered to their train stations at a specific time. Some merchants had refrigerated trucks as well, and delivered to suburban locations not served by the railroads, as well as to resorts on the New Jersey shore.

After World War II, the market fell into disrepair and occupancy dropped. The building's survival was endangered, but in 1990 the Pennsylvania Convention Center Authority purchased it from Reading and secured a $30 million public grant to upgrade the infrastructure and freshen up the interior. Historic preservationists and shoppers alike were thrilled, and now the seventy-five stalls are filled again with selections ranging from meats, poultry, and seafood to produce and spices, prepared foods, and baked goods. The market's where you'll find both Beiler's Bakery and Beiler's Donuts and Salads—not to mention the obligatory cheesesteak.

FEDERAL DONUTS

Federal Donuts doesn't have a "signature flavor." Since the first of the four current shops opened in the fall of 2011, the menu has constantly changed and evolved, which is perhaps why the loyal clientele is already waiting at the 7:00 a.m. opening. They never know when milk chocolate sea salt, sticky bun, pink lemonade, pumpkin-spiced latte, or chocolate-covered strawberry will join the ranks of maple bacon, Turkish coffee, and the other flavors that become culinary memories when the cycle rotates.

"Enjoy them while they're here, because they won't be back," says Felicia D'Ambrosio, one of the five founding partners. All of the partners had a background in the food and restaurant industry before starting Federal Donuts. The best-known name on the list is Michael Solomonov, who worked at high-end restaurants like Vetri and Striped Bass before launching Zahav, a modern Israeli restaurant, after returning from a few years in his native Israel.

Federal does only cake donuts, and it features three simple ones that are fried to order, as well as six fancy glazed flavors at a time, cycling options off the menu every few weeks. The shops open early, with the cases stocked, but they close when the last donut is gone.

The simple donuts are a favorite with kids, but "simple" is hardly synonymous with "boring." The freshly fried donuts are sprinkled with interesting topping combinations: brown sugar cinnamon,

1219 S. Second Street
(267) 687-8258

1362 Sansom Street
(215) 665-1101

3428 Sansom Street
(267) 275-8489

701 N. Seventh Street
(267) 928-3893

www.federaldonuts.com

powdered vanilla mixed with lavender and cocoa scented with orange zest among others.

But the shop's fame is founded on the appearance and flavors of its glazed donuts. The donuts are made from flavored dough, and then embellished with glazes and garnishes. Cake donuts can be dry, but not at Federal Donuts, where the basic dough creates a masterwork of moist, rich flavor that harmonizes with the wide variety of glaze flavors.

The same sort of innovation is applied to the shops' other core food, Korean-style fried chicken. Each order is served with homemade Japanese cucumber pickles and a honey donut. What makes Korean-style fried chicken special is that it is double fried to create a light crispy coating that never becomes soggy, while the meat is succulent and moist. It's a technique that the partners learned from a local shop called Café Soho.

While it can be ordered unadorned, most of the customers flavor their fowl by selecting from one of three dry spice rubs—like buttermilk ranch or dill pickle—or one of three wet glazes, one of which is a variation on Thai sweet chile. As with the donuts, the demand for fried chicken always outstrips the supply on any given day, even when customers had to trudge through knee-high snow to get there. Customers stand around—Federal Donuts shops have just a few stools and no tables—clutching the slips of paper entitling them to buy a half chicken as if they were winning lottery tickets. After all, even a winning lottery ticket won't get you this kind of bliss.

Federal Donuts has four locations, plus a kiosk at the stadium (Citizens Bank Park) that is open during Phillies home games.

FEDERAL DONUT'S GINGERBREAD GLAZE

Makes 1 cup

3 tablespoons brewed coffee

2 tablespoons fresh ginger juice

1 tablespoon dark molasses

¼ teaspoon ground cinnamon

Pinch of ground cloves

Pinch of salt

2 cups confectioners' sugar

BECAUSE THERE are no repeats on the menu, this glaze—which is perfect as a topping for sugar cookies as well as donuts—is a distant memory at Federal Donuts. But you can enjoy it at home.

Combine the coffee, ginger juice, molasses, cinnamon, cloves, and salt in a heatproof mixing bowl. Set it over a saucepan of simmering water and stir. Whisk until smooth.

Continuing to work over the simmering water, slowly whisk in the confectioners' sugar, stirring until the sugar melts and the glaze is smooth. Scrape the glaze into a shallow bowl and allow it to cool before dipping donuts.

The glaze can be prepared up to 4 hours in advance and kept at room temperature. Press a sheet of plastic wrap directly into the surface to keep it from hardening.

The easiest way to get fresh ginger juice is to put slices of ginger through a garlic press. It is not necessary to peel the ginger, but it should be thinly sliced to extract the most juice.

FRANGELLI'S BAKERY

For John Colosi, owning Frangelli's Bakery fulfills a childhood dream. He grew up in a row house in South Philly that was right across the street from the shop. He'd smell the donuts cooking. His father used to take him for ice cream donuts—stuffed with handmade Neapolitan block ice cream—in the summer and jelly donuts in the winter.

John, a former construction worker, purchased the bakery from Anthony Frangelli, the son of founder Tony Frangelli, in 2010. The purchase included Tony's original recipes for both his yeast-raised donuts and his Italian pastry cream, so the same recipes have been prepared at this unassuming spot since 1947.

While the bakery makes a full line of European and Italian pastries, including cannoli and butter cookies, it became known early on for its donuts. "Everything is filled to order," says John. "We use a very expensive black raspberry jelly in the jelly donuts, and we make our own glazes and fillings for the filled donuts and long johns. Customers watch as ladies behind the counter use a pumping machine to custom-make each one."

John explains: "We want the donut shells themselves to remain warm because we make them all through the day, and pre-filled donuts can become soggy." And filling them to order also means that customers have the opportunity to top them with their glaze of choice or an avalanche of confectioners' sugar.

Frangelli's Bakery
847 West Ritner Street
Philadelphia, Pennsylvania 19148
(215) 271-7878

www.frangellis.com

One new addition to Frangelli's offerings is creating quite a stir in the local media. In 2013 John introduced a donut-cannoli hybrid. While he first dubbed it a "Donnoli," it has now been personally branded as the "Franolli."

One day, John explains, he had just finished making the sweetened ricotta cheese filling for cannoli, and he spied an unfilled donut next to him. "I was actually a bit hungry, so I filled the donut with it and really enjoyed it," he says. He then made a few to have the staff sample, and when they gave it a rave review, he tried it out on customers, who joined in the cheers. Franollis are now made daily.

In addition to donuts, Frangelli's also makes crullers, glazed with either chocolate or vanilla. In the fall there are pumpkin donuts, and there are fruit flavors in the summer. During the fall and winter, the shop ramps up production because customers are no longer spending weekends at the beach.

John revived the custom of ice cream donuts in 2011, and he now makes his own dense fudgy chocolate ice cream as well as filling donuts with the classic Neapolitan.

PEACE, LOVE & LITTLE DONUTS

Marci and Ron Razete, the founders of Peace, Love & Little Donuts, were both born in 1960 and they embrace the whimsy of the VW bus with tie-dyed curtains and the bright colors of the '60s and '70s. It's their spirit of fun that inspired the motto of their business, started in 2009: "Feed Your Inner Hippie."

Hippies of all ages have been doing just that. The donuts are little; they're less than three inches in diameter. So there is little, if any, guilt involved in eating a few at a sitting.

What is now an asset and marketing tool for their donuts began from necessity. Ron assembled the machine they use to extrude and fry the donuts incorrectly. The donuts emerged little, and in a "go with the flow" attitude, they accepted that as how it was supposed to be.

All of the donuts at Peace, Love & Little Donuts are variations on cake, and they are made continually during the day so customers are assured of a fresh, warm donut. While the shop makes a mean brownie-textured devil's food donut, as well as excellent blueberry and red velvet dough, it's the old-fashioned sour cream donut that is the most popular, because it can be enhanced in so many ways. During the fall and winter, cider and pumpkin donuts are also on the menu.

The donuts fall into a few categories, depending on the way they are finished and decorated. Groovy Donuts are all dipped in homemade granulated sugar flavored with everything from ginger

2018 Smallman Street
Pittsburgh, Pennsylvania 15222
(412) 904-4649

100 Broughton Road
Bethel Park, Pennsylvania 15201
(313) 4-DONUTS

www.peaceloveandlittledonuts.com

to cinnamon to maple. One step up the line are the Far Out Donuts, all of which are frosted. In addition to the chocolate, vanilla, and strawberry basics, frosting flavors include mocha, lemon, banana, and orange cream cheese. Funkadelic Donuts are frosted donuts with all sorts of toppings. In addition to the ubiquitous maple bacon combination, try sprinkles, coconut, crushed M&M's, or cherry cheesecake. And on the top rung of the Peace, Love & Little Donuts ladder are the Signature Donuts. These most-unusual options include lemon ginger, pineapple upside-down cake, piña colada, and raspberry lemonade.

The first shop is in downtown Pittsburgh's Strip District, which was a concentration of produce wholesalers in the early nineteenth century and is now an area filled with independent restaurants and food businesses. In the summer of 2014, Marci and Ron opened a second shop in nearby Bethel Park.

But there are Peace, Love & Little Donuts outlets in places as far-flung as Florida and Oregon.

Ron refers to them as "licensees" rather than "franchisees." "While there are many aspects of both models that overlap, a key difference to us is that we don't put down a prospectus that anyone can buy and open up a franchise," says Ron. "We get people coming to us who have fallen in love with our little donuts and what we do and really want to let people in their part of the country enjoy it."

Ron shares the proprietary recipes and techniques with the new shops, and all of them invite customers to Feed Your Inner Hippie.

Peace, Love & Little Donuts has two locations owned and run by Marci and Ron.

FRACTURED PRUNE DOUGHNUTS

★ OCEAN CITY, MARYLAND, AND OTHER LOCATIONS ★

There are a lot of specialty donuts on the menu at Fractured Prune shops. They range from Blackberry Cobbler (topped with blackberry glaze sprinkled generously with graham cracker crumbs and confectioners' sugar) and French Toast (coated with maple glaze and sprinkled with coarse cinnamon sugar) to Banana Cream Pie (glistening with a banana glaze sprinkled with crushed vanilla wafers and cinnamon sugar) and Carnival (with a thick coating of rainbow sprinkles adhered to the honey glaze).

But what makes this chain, which is now going national with franchises, unique is that the donuts can be personalized and that they're always made to order so they're put in your hands hot. The motto is "We don't just serve donuts, we serve an experience."

On hand at all times are nineteen glazes and thirteen toppings, and they can be combined any way a customer wants them. Everyone starts with a basic vanilla cake donut; you can't decide you

want a donut flavored with mint or melon. But if you want mint as a glaze and a sprinkling of miniature chocolate chips, your wish is their command. The second catchphrase used by the shops is "You create 'em. We make 'em."

The name Fractured Prune relates to a colorful character in Ocean City history. Prunella Shriek was somewhat of a late-nineteenth century feminist who liked to compete in men's sporting events—even when in her seventies. She was always returning home either on crutches or in a wheelchair, and the townspeople started calling her Fractured Prunella. The logo shows a prune sporting sunglasses (appropriate for the shop's beach location) with a mug of coffee in one arm and the other one in a sling.

The insistence on serving donuts hot is what led to the growth of the Fractured Prune; that meant that donuts had to be made as they were being ordered. The transition from one shop to many in Ocean Springs began when Sandy Tyler, and her daughter and son-in-law, Colleen and Ted Kaufman, bought the name and equipment from the first owner in 1992.

The donuts are mixed by hand, and then formed into perfect circles and fried up by a robotic machine that can create more than eight hundred donuts an hour. Colleen was in charge of creating the glazes, and all other hands turn into a production line to fill orders.

The glazes include the traditional honey, chocolate, and maple, and also more unusual options like banana, peanut butter, and cherry. Bacon bits are among the toppings—should someone have not yet encountered a maple bacon donut—plus all sorts of candy, crushed cookies, coconut, and peanuts.

The expansion of Fractured Prune beyond its comfortable enclave on the Atlantic coast came about in 2013, when Dan Brinton, who had been a Krispy Kreme franchisee for seventeen years, purchased it from Sandy and the Kaufmans.

127th Street
Ocean City, Maryland 21842
(410) 250-4400

81st Street and Coastal Highway
Ocean City, Maryland 21842
(410) 524-4688

2808 Philadelphia Avenue
Ocean City, Maryland 21842
(410) 289-1134

On the Boardwalk
306 South Atlantic Avenue
Ocean City, Maryland 21842

9636 Stephen Decatur Highway
West Ocean City, Maryland 21842
(410) 213-9799

www.fracturedprune.com

There are already shops in Arizona, Michigan, and Utah, and he promises, "we'll be expanding more on the West coast in the years to come." He says that only about 30 percent of the customers take advantage of the ability to customize donuts (rather than order a pre-designed specialty) early in the morning, but that percentage increases later in the day and on weekends.

"As the father of three young kids, it's wonderful to watch their faces light up when you tell them what they can choose from," says Dan.

There are now about fifty Fractured Prune shops, with the majority clustered in the Mid-Atlantic states near beaches. Listed above are the addresses of the Ocean City locations, where it all began.

CHOCOLATE GANACHE GLAZE

Makes 2 cups

½ pound good-quality bittersweet chocolate, finely chopped

1 cup confectioners' sugar

Pinch of salt

½ teaspoon pure vanilla extract

1 cup heavy cream

1 tablespoon unsalted butter

THIS RICH, intensely flavored chocolate glaze is like the one prepared at Fractured Prune donut shops. It can also be drizzled on ice cream or over cake.

Combine the chocolate, sugar, and salt in a mixing bowl. Combine the vanilla, cream, and butter in a small saucepan and bring to a simmer over low heat, stirring frequently.

Pour the cream over the chocolate and allow to sit for 2 minutes without stirring. Whisk the mixture until smooth. Allow to cool to a spreadable consistency before dipping donuts.

If not using the glaze within a few hours, press a sheet of plastic wrap directly into the surface to prevent it from hardening.

VARIATIONS: Omit the vanilla and add 1 tablespoon of Grand Marnier or Triple Sec and 2 teaspoons grated orange zest to the glaze.

Add 1 tablespoon of instant espresso powder or instant coffee granules to the cream mixture.

ASTRO DOUGHNUTS & FRIED CHICKEN

Every American has childhood donut memories, and for Jeff Halpern and Elliot Spaisman, they center on a shop in suburban Maryland where their parents took them after hockey practice. The two men, now in their mid-thirties, remained friends and followed separate career paths until 2013, when they became co-owners of Astro Doughnuts & Fried Chicken, a storefront in the bustling Metro Center part of downtown Washington.

Jeff spent more than a decade as a professional hockey player, many of them with the Washington Capitals. Elliot, meanwhile, had traded hockey sticks for table legs, running an antique business. But both are now focused full-time on the fryers, serving up a few varieties of fried chicken alongside a dizzying array of creative donuts.

The small storefront is a place to order, grab, and go; there's even an iPhone app to make ordering easier. At downtown Washington real estate prices, Astro Doughnuts doesn't have the luxury of chairs, tables, or lingering. The donuts and chicken, in fact, are fried in the basement and sent up on a dumbwaiter. But customers can still enjoy the aroma of sweet donuts mixing with spicy chicken when they walk in the door.

Customers always find about a dozen flavors of donuts in the case. There is a lot of butter in the yeast-raised donuts; they are truly similar to rings of fried brioche. Astro's staples are the glazed, crème brûlée, maple bacon, and peanut butter and

Astro Doughnuts & Fried Chicken
1308 G Street NW
Washington, DC 20005
(202) 809-5565

www.astrodoughnuts.com

jelly donuts. Many of the donuts are monogrammed with a small letter "a" for decoration; some are square rather than the traditional round. "One of the biggest things we thought about was being able to take a bite of a donut and not have the filling fall into your lap, and the square accomplishes that," says Jeff.

Pastry chef Elizabeth Masetti is also very aware of the importance of textural variation in the donut-eating experience. Many of the donuts are thickly encrusted with toppings that include nuts, cookie crumbs, chopped chocolate, and *fleur de sel*.

Then the options change daily, monthly, and seasonally. In the spring there's a special donut to honor the Cherry Blossom Festival: It's filled with black cherry compote and has Earl Grey tea infused in the glaze. In the fall and winter, the options tend to be more geared to warm flavors like pumpkin and gingerbread, and are more likely to be cake donuts than yeast. Fruit flavors dominate the spring and summer rotations.

Not all the donuts are sweet, however. The crossover option joining the donut and chicken sides of the menu is a fried chicken BLT made with Benton's bacon sandwiched between halves of chive and cheddar donut. There's also a Buffalo chicken sandwich served on a plain donut with blue cheese dressing.

The fried chicken comes in two different preparations. There's a classic buttermilk served with roasted potato salad with bacon from the American South, and then there's a twice-fried Korean chicken served with crunchy Asian slaw from the south of that peninsula (it's served with a choice of fiery sriracha glaze or spicy garlic glaze).

There are options for enjoying the donuts that don't include a ride on the Metro. In January 2014, Astro began selling donuts from its own food truck that makes the rounds in Northern Virginia, and on weekends they're on offer at Dean & DeLuca's tiny Georgetown market.

BRIOCHE DONUTS

Makes 12 to 14

4 teaspoons active dry yeast

½ cup whole milk, heated to 110°F to 115°F

¼ cup granulated sugar

3½ cups all-purpose flour, divided, plus more for dusting

4 large eggs, at room temperature

¾ teaspoon salt

1 cup (2 sticks) unsalted butter, very soft, sliced

Vegetable oil for frying

HERE IS ONE DONUT that, due to the amount of butter in the dough, tastes sinfully rich without a filling. There's very little sugar in the dough, however, so this donut would be at home with a savory filling like the Buffalo chicken and bleu cheese dressing made at Astro. The donuts are also delicious with just about any glaze or filling to glorify them.

Combine the yeast, milk, sugar, and ½ cup flour in the bowl of a stand mixer fitted with the paddle attachment, and mix well. Set aside for about 10 minutes while the yeast proofs.

When the yeast looks frothy, add the eggs, one at a time, and beat well. Add the remaining flour and salt, and beat at low speed until the flour is incorporated, forming a soft dough. Beat the dough for 5 minutes at medium speed. Add the butter, a few slices at a time, while beating the dough at medium speed. Allow the butter to be absorbed into the dough before adding more.

Place the dough hook on the mixer, and knead the dough at medium speed for 2 minutes. Raise the speed to high, and knead for an additional 3 to 4 minutes, or until the dough forms a soft ball and is springy. (If kneading by hand, this will take about 10 to 12 minutes.)

Lightly grease the inside of a large mixing bowl with softened butter or vegetable oil. Add the dough, turning it so it is lightly greased all over. Cover the bowl loosely with a sheet of oiled plastic wrap or a damp tea towel, and place it in a warm, draft-free spot. Allow the dough to rise for 1 to 2 hours, or until it has doubled in bulk.

Punch the dough down, and cover the bowl with plastic wrap. Refrigerate the dough overnight to develop the flavor.

Line a baking sheet with parchment paper or a silicone baking mat. Punch the dough down. Dust a surface and rolling pin with flour. Roll the dough to a thickness of ¾ inch. Use a donut cutter

(recipe continues)

dipped in flour to cut out as many donuts as possible; alternatively, use a 3-inch cookie cutter and then cut out holes with a ¾-inch cutter. Reroll the scraps one time to a thickness of ¾ inch and cut out more donuts and holes. Transfer the donuts to the baking sheet.

Cover the baking sheet with a sheet of oiled plastic wrap, and let donuts rise in a warm place until doubled in bulk, about 30 to 40 minutes.

Heat at least 2 inches of oil to a temperature of 350°F in a Dutch oven or deep skillet. Place a few layers of paper towels on a baking sheet and top it with a wire cooling rack.

Carefully slide a few donuts into the hot oil, being careful not to crowd the pan and making sure that the donuts do not touch each other. Once the donuts float to the top of the oil, fry them for 1 minute. Gently flip them over using a wire mesh spoon or a chopstick, and fry for an additional 1 to 1¼ minutes, or until evenly browned.

Drain the donuts on the rack, blotting them gently with additional paper towels. Fry the remaining donuts and the donut holes in the same manner.

The cut-out donuts can be refrigerated for up to 4 hours. When ready to cook, allow them to complete their rising if they have not yet doubled in bulk. Fry them just prior to serving.

DISTRICT DOUGHNUT

Now operating out of a shop across from the iconic Marine Barracks on Capitol Hill, District Doughnut gained a huge following as a stealth organization delivering donuts to functions and coffee shops for two years before moving into a brick-and-mortar space in the fall of 2014. It was during this period that Christine Schaefer perfected her inventive yeast-raised donut dough. It draws from her background as a Cordon Bleu–trained pastry chef who ran a gourmet bakery in Buffalo, New York, before moving to Washington.

Her donuts are global favorites turned into donut form. The donuts are on the relatively small side; they're about three inches in diameter. Customers find that their petite size means you can eat a few of them at one time to experience the range of subtle flavors.

One of the founding partners of District Doughnut is Juan Pablo Segura, whose parents moved to the area from their native Argentina. The dulce de leche donut reflects his heritage, while the caramel apple streusel donut, with bits of sautéed Granny Smith apple rolled right into the cinnamon-scented dough and topped with caramel and a butter streusel topping, is the all-American favorite of the other partner, Greg Menna. The two men, now in their late twenties, have been friends since the sixth grade, and they say they bonded over donuts.

Customer favorites include a brown butter donut drawn from the French pastry tradition,

District Doughnut
749 8th Street SE
Washington, DC 20003
(202) 817-3166

www.districtdoughnuts.com

with a glaze made with nutty brown butter drizzled over a cinnamon and sugar coating, and the cannoli donut, in which sweetened ricotta cheese flecked with chocolate fills vanilla bean–flavored dough dusted with confectioners' sugar and cocoa powder.

"We're the donut that America deserves," says Greg. He says that the donuts appeal to a sophisticated palate and contain very little sugar so that the identification of the various flavors is not clouded.

The dough itself is individualized to become part of the flavor profile. There is fresh orange zest folded into the dough for the orange chocolate donut, and the cream filling is made with reduced fresh orange juice, which is also added to the chocolate ganache glaze. While other donut shops are using their blowtorches to create a crispy brûlée topping, at District Doughnut, one browns delicate fluffy peaks crowning a lemon meringue donut (tart-sweet lemon curd is encased in lemon zest–flavored dough).

District Doughnut became known through a two-year marketing effort that focused on food festivals and large corporate events, as well as selling to Uncommon Grounds, the Georgetown University student-owned coffee shop. Individual donuts were hawked via social media: When Greg was making a corporate delivery, he would bring extra donuts along and post his location on Twitter.

During these years of experimentation, District Doughnut operated out of a facility called Union Kitchen. Calling itself a "food incubator," the commercial kitchen, fully licensed by the Board of Health, allows small food business to test the viability of their ideas without incurring debt or signing leases. District Doughnut shared the space and equipment with more than fifty other start-up businesses, ranging from coffee roasters and charcuterie makers to bakers and food trucks.

BROWN BUTTER GLAZE

Makes 1 cup

½ cup (1 stick) unsalted butter, sliced

2 to 3 tablespoons whole milk, divided

½ teaspoon pure vanilla extract

¼ teaspoon ground cinnamon

¼ teaspoon ground ginger

2 cups confectioners' sugar

THE NUTTINESS of aromatic brown butter is truly alluring. It's highlighted by the inclusion of ginger and cinnamon in this easy glaze that is excellent for all donuts.

Heat the butter in a saucepan over medium heat for 6 to 8 minutes or until golden brown, swirling the pan by its handle but not stirring the butter. Watch carefully—butter can go from golden brown to burned black very quickly.

Carefully pour the butter into a shallow mixing bowl, leaving the brown sediment behind. Whisk in 2 tablespoons of the milk, along with the vanilla, cinnamon, and ginger. Add the confectioners' sugar slowly, whisking constantly, until the mixture is smooth. Add additional milk, a few drops at a time, if the glaze seems too thick for dipping. Use immediately, or press a sheet of plastic wrap directly into the surface to keep it from hardening.

The glaze can be prepared up to 4 hours in advance and kept at room temperature.

The farm-to-table movement is one of the most exciting trends of this century, with chefs from all over the country forging relationships with farmers and fishermen in their regions to ensure the freshness of the seasonal ingredients on their menus. In the Washington area, "farm to table" has a second meaning. Some of the most popular new restaurants in the region are owned and operated by the North Dakota Farmers Union, which boasts more than 40,000 members.

One of these, located in Georgetown on the banks of the Potomac River, is Farmers Fishers Bakers, a huge restaurant seating more than two hundred. That's where pastry chef Ashley Soto produces thousands of the group's signature donuts, Uncle Buck's Beignets.

Named for one of the group's founders, the beignets are not from the New Orleans tradition of yeast-raised beignets; they are made with *pâte à choux*. If the pastry is piped out into a circle, it's called a French cruller (page 24), and if it's baked, it becomes a cream puff or profiterole. But when it's dropped from a spoon into the hot fat to fry, it's a beignet. The donuts are coated with confectioners' sugar and served with a trio of sweet dipping sauces: hot fudge, bourbon caramel, and raspberry.

And luckily for diners, they're always available, beginning in the morning at First Bake, at which casual baked goods and beverages are

Farmers Fishers Bakers
3000 K Street NW
Washington, DC 20007
(202) 298-TRUE (8783)

www.farmersfishersbakers.com

served in the Larder, a room housing colorful jars of pickles and preserves featured on the menu. They play a role on the brunch menu as both a starter and a dessert, and then act as dessert at other meals. All the beignets are cooked to order, and diners are informed that there is a short wait time.

While Uncle Buck's Beignets are always available, there are also other donuts on the menu periodically, including brioche-style yeast donuts and maple bacon donuts served alongside fried chicken.

The menu at Farmers Fishers Bakers is huge and varied. It would be impossible for anyone to not find something that appeals to them, including vegetarians and vegans. Executive chef Joe Goetze designed a menu that is really unstructured. It's possible to eat a traditional three-course meal with an appetizer, entrée, and dessert. But it's also possible to have a light meal or for a group to share a number of different options—from pizzas and sliders to homemade pretzels served with pimento cheese and barbecue mustard to hot crab dip and calamari.

The first word in the name of the restaurant is "Farmers," and, as you would expect, there are a number of creative salads, ranging from shaved cauliflower and Asian pear to fried Brussels sprouts sprinkled with blue cheese. The "Fishers" portion of the menu runs the gamut from ginger planked salmon to more than one way to fry a fish, and a whole section of the menu is devoted to various preparations of steamed mussels. Of course there are meats, with an emphasis on beef and pork, and a whole meatless section with options like mushroom Reuben and veggie "meatloaf."

The interior of the restaurant is loaded with whimsical touches, such as real wheat embedded in the resin of the bar, and a tangerine-painted cow standing on a shelf hanging from the ceiling. And men might look a bit unnerved when they exit the bathroom. It's "decorated" with an implement used for castrating bulls as a way of emphasizing neatness when in the space.

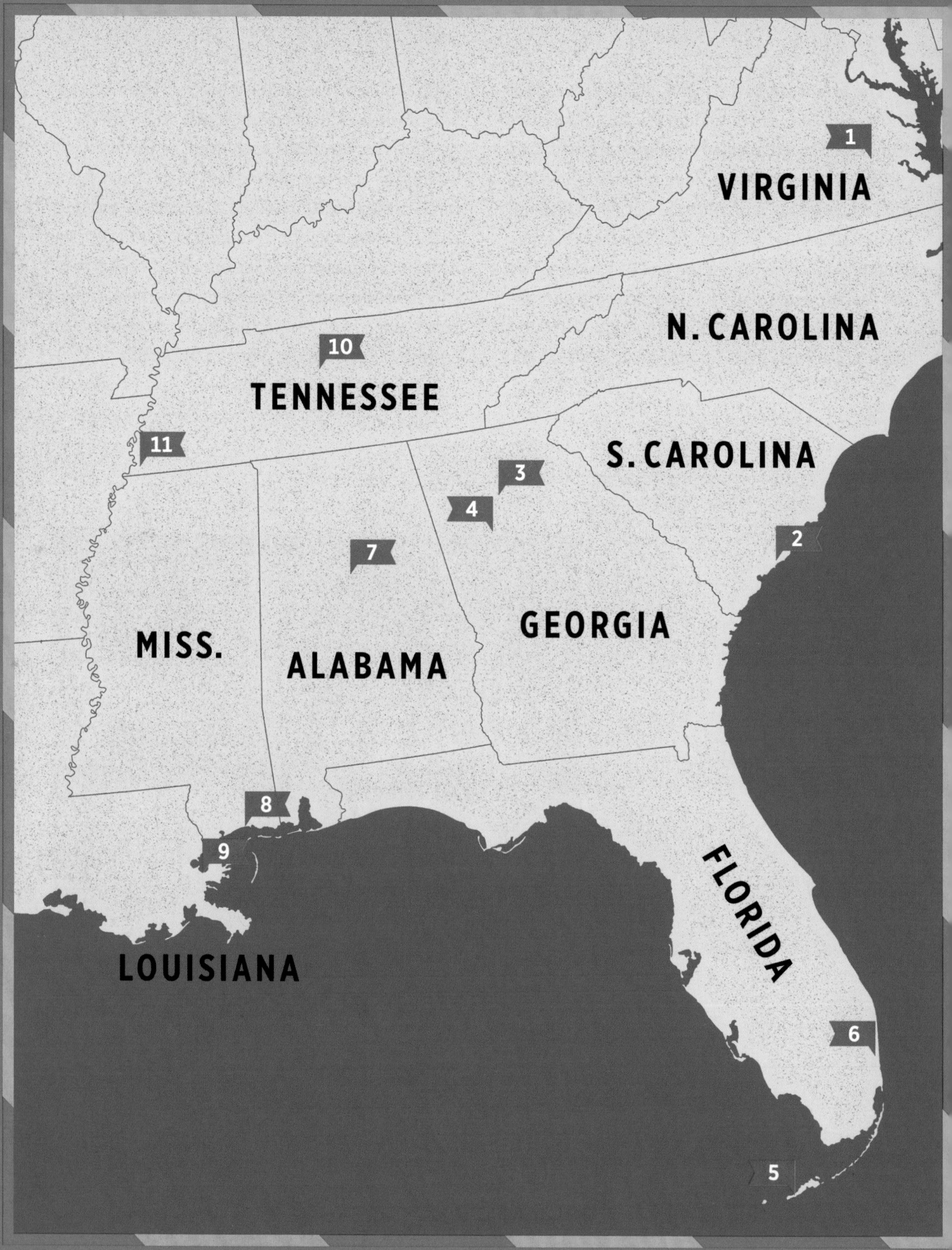

VIRGINIA

N. CAROLINA

S. CAROLINA

TENNESSEE

GEORGIA

MISS.

ALABAMA

FLORIDA

LOUISIANA

1

2

3

4

5

6

7

8

9

10

11

Chapter 3

THE SOUTHERN STATES

Donuts have an innate appeal to Southerners, as the South is one region of the country that doesn't have reservations about fried foods. From chicken and hush puppies to fried pies, there's a natural affinity for that inimitable fried texture south of the Mason-Dixon Line.

The South was the region that spawned Krispy Kreme, when founder Vernon Rudolph opened a plant in Winston-Salem, North Carolina, in 1937 and began selling donuts to supermarkets. Very soon his donuts became a regional standard, and to this day, many independent donut shops feel that they are still trying to top that popular standard.

Many Southern donuts take advantage of the cornucopia of fruits that grow here, from peaches and strawberries to key limes and mangoes.

1. SUGAR SHACK DONUTS
2. GLAZED GOURMET DOUGHNUTS
3. DUTCH MONKEY DOUGHNUTS
4. SUBLIME DOUGHNUTS
5. GLAZED DONUTS & COFFEE
6. RHINO DOUGHNUTS & COFFEE
7. THE HEAVENLY DONUT COMPANY
8. THE TATONUT SHOP
9. CAFÉ DU MONDE
10. FOX'S DONUT DEN
11. GIBSON'S DONUTS

SUGAR SHACK DONUTS

There's a constant surprise factor awaiting customers at Sugar Shack Donuts. The cooks on duty get to decide what they want to make, and the flavors can change every five to ten minutes.

A sign at the shop lists the "permanent menu." This includes the classics, like chocolate iced and glazed, and the new classics, like maple bacon and Samoa-style, along with fruit fritters. At some point in the day, most of these will make an appearance in the case.

But on other occasions, the flavors have included espresso iced, toasted sunflower seeds, bourbon walnut, lavender honey, fresh mint, and cilantro lime. In addition to topping maple iced donuts with bits of bacon, occasionally the shop will work in tandem with Lee's Famous Recipe Chicken, a Richmond institution, and top donuts with nuggets of fried chicken breast.

Some mornings there might even be breakfast sandwiches on split-open long johns. These could be vegetarian options, like goat cheese and oyster mushrooms, or heartier fare, like scrambled eggs with ham and cheese.

And this is the way that owner Ian Kelley, now just 30 years old, envisioned the shop working. Ian's career followed an almost European path, featuring a number of apprenticeships as a teenager rather than enrollment in culinary school. In 2004, when Ian was just 19, he was already part-owner of the Old City Bar in downtown Richmond. In 2007, he sold his interest in the fine dining restaurant and everything he owned, packed up his van, and hit the road.

He worked in Colorado at an upscale Italian restaurant, and then at a French bistro in Seattle, where he learned to fry up beignets. He also became aware of such donut shops as Top Pot in Seattle (page 233) and Voodoo in Portland (page 228). "Richmond is really a foodie town, and I just knew that the people would respond to these types of donuts," he says. He returned to Richmond and purchased a former used car lot in 2012. The first Sugar Shack opened in June 2013.

Part of what Ian had learned on his West Coast career odyssey was that people had to have their own creativity encouraged to stay excited in a professional kitchen. So the ever-changing menu was always part of Ian's plan. "I'm not into the robotic thing of doing the same thing all the time," he says.

But necessity also factored in. "The day we opened I had a set menu and took it off the wall two hours later. We couldn't keep up with the demand and I told the cooks to just start making

1001 North Lombardy Street
Richmond, Virginia 23220
(804) 278-5900

1110 East Main Street
Richmond, Virginia 23219
(804) 225-0700

1501 Parham Road
Richmond, Virginia 23229
(804) 288-1200

whatever donuts they wanted to make," he says, recalling the chaos.

At first there were no jelly donuts, because Ian wanted to perfect the recipe, and all of the fruit glazes are now made with fresh seasonal fruits. Ian worked the kinks out at his first shop, and he then opened a second in downtown Richmond in February 2014. By the end of the year, Sugar Shack had expanded north to the Old Town district of Alexandria and into Charlottesville, home of the University of Virginia.

Ian believes that with his extensive training programs the quality of the donuts at all shops will be consistent. And he's hiring staff who like to "do their own thing and create fun and delicious donuts."

JELLY DONUTS

Makes 12 to 14

2½ teaspoons active
dry yeast

¼ cup granulated sugar

1 cup whole milk, heated to
110°F to 115°F, divided

4 to 4½ cups bread flour,
divided, plus more for dusting

½ teaspoon salt

2 large eggs, beaten

3 tablespoons unsalted
butter, melted and cooled

Vegetable oil for frying

1½ cups jam or jelly
of your choice

½ cup confectioners' sugar

WHILE IAN KELLEY didn't serve jelly donuts at first, they're now a fixture on his menu. This recipe is the utility infielder of yeast-raised donuts. It's foolproof, and you can keep the fried donuts in the freezer and then fill them and dust them with confectioners' sugar in a matter of minutes.

Combine the yeast, sugar, ½ cup warm milk, and ⅓ cup of the flour in the bowl of a stand mixer fitted with the paddle attachment, and mix well. Set aside for about 10 minutes while the yeast proofs.

When the yeast looks frothy, add the remaining milk, remaining flour, salt, eggs, and butter. Beat at low speed until the flour is incorporated, forming a soft dough.

Place the dough hook on the mixer, and knead the dough at medium speed for 2 minutes. Raise the speed to high, and knead for an additional 3 to 4 minutes, or until the dough forms a soft ball and is springy. (If kneading by hand, this will take about 10 to 12 minutes.)

Lightly grease the inside of a large mixing bowl with softened butter or vegetable oil. Add the dough, turning it so it is lightly greased all over. Cover the bowl loosely with a sheet of oiled plastic wrap or a damp tea towel, and place it in a warm, draft-free spot. Allow the dough to rise for 1 to 2 hours, or until it has doubled in bulk.

Punch down the risen dough. Line a baking sheet with parchment paper or a silicone baking mat. Dust a surface and rolling pin generously with flour. Scrape the dough onto the surface and knead it gently for 30 seconds. Roll the dough into a circle ½ inch thick. Cut out as many donuts as possible with a 3-inch donut cutter, dipped in flour and gently transfer the rounds to the baking sheet with a floured spatula. Reroll the scraps one time to a thickness of ½ inch and cut out more donuts. Cover the baking sheet with a sheet of oiled plastic wrap and let the donuts rise for 20 minutes, or until doubled in bulk.

(recipe continues)

Heat at least 2 inches of oil to a temperature of 350°F in a Dutch oven or deep skillet. Place a few layers of paper towels on a baking sheet and top it with a wire cooling rack.

Carefully slide a few donuts into the hot oil, being careful not to crowd the pan and making sure that the donuts do not touch each other. Once the donuts float to the top of the oil, fry them for 1 to 1½ minutes. Gently flip them over using a wire mesh spoon or a chopstick, and fry for an additional 1 minute, or until they are evenly browned.

Drain the donuts on the rack, blotting them gently with additional paper towels. Fry the remaining donuts and the donut holes in the same manner.

When the donuts are cooled, place the jam or jelly in a pastry bag fitted with a ½-inch tip and insert 2 tablespoons through the side of each donut into the center. Sift confectioners' sugar over the filled donuts, and serve immediately.

You can let the donuts rise for the second time refrigerated; this will take about 4 to 6 hours. Fry them and fill them just prior to serving.

GLAZED GOURMET DOUGHNUTS

★ CHARLESTON, SOUTH CAROLINA ★

It's not often that the menu at a donut shop prompts adjectives like "adventurous," but then few donut shops feature flavors like chocolate curry spiked with crystallized ginger, add chipotle peppers as an accent to a chocolate orange glaze, or top an apple-filled donut with a thin slice of crisply baked cheddar cheese.

Glazed Gourmet, which hung its white round sign up in October 2011, is the brainchild of Charleston native Allison Smith and her boyfriend, Mark Remi, an Indonesian-born computer engineer. A year earlier, Allison was finishing up her studies at Charleston's Culinary Institute and looking for a hole to fill among the city's wide range of excellent bakeries. She decided that it was in the nascent niche of artisan donuts.

Glazed Gourmet Doughnuts
481 King Street
Charleston, South Carolina 29403
(843) 577-5557

www.glazedgourmet.com

Allison and Mark visited such bastions as Doughnut Plant in New York (page 64) and Dynamo Donut + Coffee in San Francisco (page 217), and then she went to work on her recipes. "I knew a lot about the chemistry of baking, but I had no real experience working with donuts," Allison says. A few hundred pounds of flour later, she was finally happy with her light and fluffy yeast-raised recipe, and she had invented about a dozen cake donut flavors, too.

Her signature donut is the Purple Goat, filled with a combination of berries and goat cheese. In addition to the ubiquitous maple bacon, she also makes a bacon apple fritter. The Charleston, flavored with bourbon and topped with bits of crunchy praline, is included in all the donut weddings she caters because "it's such a great representation of the city." Another liquor-laced favorite is the Italian, a donut filled with Frangelico pastry cream and topped with a toffee glaze and toasted almonds.

Glazed Gourmet draws from a wide range of herbs and spices for its flavoring arsenal along with fruits, nuts, and—of course—chocolate. One of Allison's personal favorites is a pastry cream filling made with cardamom. Donut holes are dusted with Chinese five-spice powder, and there's fresh basil enlivening the lime glaze on a strawberry cake donut. Many of the fruits and herbs are grown in a garden located behind the shop, and Allison sources products locally as much as possible.

While the pair would like to start a second shop, she says that she's still having "too much fun experimenting with flavor and texture combinations." And she's apparently doing it quite well. Glazed Gourmet Doughnuts has twice been selected as the best bakery in the city.

And its fame is growing nationally as well. The food and travel site Thrillist selected Glazed Gourmet for its list of the "21 Best Donut Shops in America" in the spring of 2014, and that praise followed its selection a few months earlier by Zagat as the best donut in South Carolina. According to Thrillist, "Glazed is a perfect example of the rise of the nouveau donut shop—a place where a true culinary talent uses in-house ingredients made from scratch to elevate the former cop-joke-only foodstuff to quite a lofty place."

DUTCH MONKEY DOUGHNUTS

★ CUMMING, GEORGIA ★

Power couple Arpana Satyu and Martin Burge moved to Cumming from New York in 2007 to be close to her family. Both took jobs as chefs at restaurants in the swanky Buckhead section of Atlanta, which, says Martin, is "about twenty-five minutes from Cumming on a good day."

The couple decided they didn't want to commute more than ten minutes to work, so they opened their donut shop, Dutch Monkey Doughnuts, in the village. "We lived here and thought it was absurd that we had to drive a half hour to find a good donut," says Martin. But now they're thrilled that their customers do just that, because the majority of them do trek the almost forty miles from Atlanta. With good reason, if you really love donuts.

The name of the shop, which opened in 2009, was chosen on a flight of whimsy. "We threw words around and because the origin of donuts is Dutch, that was one of them," says Arpana. Their daughter, who was two at the time, was affectionately called Monkey. Thus the name was born. The logo shows a very cute female monkey smiling as she munches on a treat.

About 75 percent of the donuts start with a yeast base. These include the lemon meringue donut filled with rich lemon curd and topped with browned meringue; the Nutella twist, a braid of dough filled with homemade chocolate hazelnut spread and sprinkled with confectioners' sugar; and the signature Dutch Monkey, overflowing with dulce de leche cream and featuring slices

Dutch Monkey Doughnuts
3075 Ronald Reagan Boulevard
Cumming, Georgia 30041
(404) 482-3650

www.dutchmonkeydoughnuts.com

of banana underneath a thick layer of chocolate ganache.

Dutch Monkey takes the now-familiar maple bacon donut to a new level by slathering it with maple cream, and bacon also appears with chocolate in the Aztec bar and serves as a foil to pineapple, jalapeño peppers, and queso fresco in a fritter. Arpana draws from her pastry chef background to create exotic combinations like a passion fruit–filled donut topped with coconut meringue and fresh lime zest, and a salted caramel long john decorated with a crosshatch of chocolate.

The remaining donuts are cake donuts made from a rotating list of seasonal favorites, many flavored with vegetables as well as fruits. Dutch Monkey has used zucchini, carrots, butternut squash, sweet potato, and spinach to add moisture to various donuts. A customer favorite remains an old-fashioned buttermilk donut. The fruits worked seasonally into both the cake dough and the glazes range from blueberries to peaches to cherries.

The shop truly makes the donuts the stars. The walls are coral and chalkboard decals on them list the contents of the case. But unlike most bakeries that arrange neat shelves by flavor, Arpana and Martin create a still life of donuts elevated onto cake stands and arranged decoratively on platters in the spacious central case.

In New York the couple worked for a pantheon of award-winning restaurants. Martin, a graduate of the Culinary Institute of America, spent the majority of his career at Gotham Bar and Grill. After a stint owning his own restaurant, Fresh, he went to work at an Italian trattoria, Vento, which is where he met Arpana. She was a graduate of the French Culinary Institute and had worked as a pastry chef for both Bobby Flay at the Mesa Grill and at Tom Colicchio's original Craft Restaurant. On one of their first dates, they ended up at a donut shop. Perhaps it was fate along with serendipity that brought them to Cumming.

LEMON CURD

Makes 3 cups

1 lemon, washed

1 cup freshly squeezed lemon juice

1½ cups granulated sugar

Pinch of salt

4 large eggs

1 cup (2 sticks) unsalted butter, cut into small pieces

LEMON MERINGUE DONUTS at Dutch Monkey Doughnuts are yeast-raised donuts with this creamy rich and tart lemon filling. The meringue on top can be browned under a broiler or with a kitchen torch.

Grate the zest from the lemon, and squeeze the juice. Combine the zest and squeezed juice, lemon juice, sugar, salt, and eggs in a saucepan, and whisk well.

Add the butter to the pan, and place it over medium-low heat. Cook, whisking constantly, for 10 to 12 minutes, or until the curd is bubbling and thick. Scrape the curd into a container, and press a sheet of plastic wrap directly into the surface to keep a skin from forming. Chill until cold.

The curd can be made up to 1 week in advance and refrigerated.

VARIATION: Substitute a lime and lime juice for the lemon and lemon juice.

SUBLIME DOUGHNUTS

It takes a lot to impress a legendary food editor, so when Dana Cowin, the editor in chief of *Food & Wine* magazine, wrote that "there is no better breakfast in the world than sweets-savant Kamal Grant's fresh strawberry and cream donut," I knew that Sublime Doughnuts must be a true culinary mecca.

The strawberry donut is more of a construction than a confection: a freshly made glazed donut is split as one would divide a shortcake into halves. It's then filled with fresh strawberries glistening in a fresh strawberry glaze and sweetened whipped cream before being dusted with confectioners' sugar. It's hardly portable, and neither are Kamal's specialties, like his assortment of ice cream "burgers" layered in split yeast-raised donuts, with flavors like Oreo cream, strawberry, and peanut butter chocolate.

Kamal, an Atlanta native, always knew he wanted to be a pastry chef, but he took a circuitous route to opening Sublime Doughnuts in the fall of 2008. A decade earlier, he graduated from Marietta High School and enlisted in the navy, where he quickly earned his shipmates' kudos for the cinnamon rolls he'd bake for their breakfast. His stint in the navy also allowed him to travel extensively and taste international flavors, including candy made from rosewater in Dubai and sweet red bean soup in Singapore. From 2002 to 2004, Kamal honed his skills at the Culinary Institute of America, where he received awards from both *Chocolatier*

Sublime Doughnuts
535 10th Street NW
Atlanta, Georgia 30318
(404) 897-1801

www.sublimedoughnuts.com

and *Pastry Art & Design* magazines, and then at the American Institute of Baking.

In addition to round goodie-topped donuts, Kamal cuts out his yeast dough and cake dough in fanciful shapes. There are stars filled with orange cream, Valentine's Day chocolate hearts filled with raspberry cream, and the Atlanta cream: It's glazed with chocolate like a Boston cream, but done in a cut-out letter A. One of the shop's most popular gifts is a happy birthday box of donuts that spells out the greeting, including the celebrant's name.

The motto of Sublime Doughnuts is "eat one that's worth it," and few folks can resist the temptation. In addition to donuts, Kamal makes fritters, which include all manner of seasonal fresh fruit, and he has begun recently making flavored funnel cakes too. "Funnel cakes are wonderfully American, but they can certainly be done with a classier touch than the ones you get at a state fair," he says. Every aspect of every donut is prepared by Kamal, from the crumbled toffee to top a praline donut to the myriad fillings and glazes.

It's not just his forms, but also his flavor combinations that garner praise. Reading reviews, one hears raves about such unusual glazes as salted caramel feathered with lines of balsamic vinegar reduction, or peach-filled donuts glazed with white chocolate. Home cooks can now replicate some of these using the recipes in Kamal's book, *Homemade Doughnuts: Techniques and Recipes for Making Sublime Doughnuts in Your Home Kitchen* (Quarry Books, 2014).

In 2012, four years after opening, Sublime Doughnuts was voted "America's Best Bakery" by *Bake* magazine. That was a long way to come from the days when he'd not only cooked all the donuts and stocked the case, but also would then change into a donut costume to lure in customers.

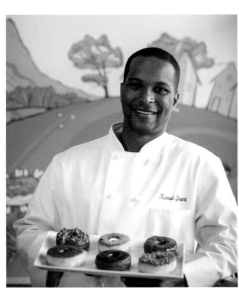

RED VELVET DONUTS WITH CREAM CHEESE ICING

Makes 12 to 15

Adapted from *Homemade Doughnuts* by Kamal Grant (Quarry Books, 2014)

DONUTS

2 cups all-purpose flour, plus more for dusting

1 tablespoon baking powder

1 teaspoon baking soda

1 teaspoon salt

1 teaspoon unsweetened cocoa powder

2 large eggs, at room temperature

½ cup granulated sugar

½ cup whole milk

2 tablespoons unsalted butter, melted and cooled

2 teaspoons liquid red food coloring

1 teaspoon pure vanilla extract

Vegetable oil for frying

ICING

4 tablespoons (½ stick) unsalted butter, softened

¼ cup (2 ounces) cream cheese, softened

1 cup confectioners' sugar

½ teaspoon pure vanilla extract

KAMAL GRANT'S red velvet donuts are very red! He doesn't pussyfoot about the amount of food coloring he adds to the dough. If you eat these light and tender donuts with your eyes closed, you'll never guess their hue—which is part of the fun if you're doing a display of donuts for a party. Kamal frosts these with old-fashioned cream cheese icing, and then tops them with a few caramelized pecans, too.

For the donuts, combine the flour, baking powder, baking soda, salt, and cocoa in a large mixing bowl and set aside. Beat the eggs at medium speed in the bowl of a stand mixer fitted with the paddle attachment, and then slowly add the sugar and increase the speed to high. Continue to beat until the mixture is thick and lemon colored.

Add the milk, butter, food coloring, and vanilla to the egg mixture, and beat well. Add the dry ingredients to the wet ingredients, and mix for 1 minute at medium speed. Chill the dough for at least 2 hours, or up to 24 hours.

Dust a surface and rolling pin heavily with flour. Roll the chilled dough to a thickness of ⅓ inch. Use a donut cutter dipped in flour to cut out as many donuts as possible; alternatively, use a 2½-inch cookie cutter and then cut out holes with a ½-inch cutter. Transfer the donuts and holes carefully to a baking sheet sprinkled with flour. Reroll the scraps one time to a thickness of ⅓ inch and cut out more donuts and holes. Allow the donuts to sit on the baking sheet for 10 minutes.

Heat at least 2 inches of oil to a temperature of 375°F in a Dutch oven or deep skillet. Place a few layers of paper towels on a baking sheet and top it with a wire cooling rack.

Carefully slide a few donuts into the hot oil, being careful not to crowd the pan and making sure that the donuts do not touch each other. Once the donuts float to the top of the oil, fry them for 1 to 1½ minutes per side, or until evenly browned.

Drain the donuts on the rack, blotting them gently with additional paper towels. Fry the remaining donuts and donut holes in the same manner. Allow the donuts to cool completely before topping them with the icing.

For the icing, combine the butter and cream cheese in a mixing bowl. Beat at high speed with a stand mixer until light and fluffy. Reduce the mixer speed to low and add the confectioners' sugar, beating until creamy. Beat in the vanilla. Top the donuts with the icing, and serve immediately.

The donuts can be cut out and refrigerated for up to 1 day, lightly covered with plastic wrap, and the icing can be made up to 2 days in advance and refrigerated. The donuts should not be fried or iced more than 6 hours prior to serving. Because of the cream cheese in the icing, any leftover donuts should be refrigerated.

Chef Kamal Grant uses a dough dispenser, a hopper into which the dough is placed so it can be pushed out in preset portions in a round shape, to form these donuts, as do almost all professional chefs. If you have one, it's not necessary to chill the dough. The purpose of chilling the dough is to stiffen it enough to roll.

GLAZED DONUTS & COFFEE

Megan and Jonathan Pidgeon, the husband and wife team who own the "southernmost donut shop in the continental United States" both graduated from the New York campus of the Culinary Institute of America in 2007. "I was tired of being cold, so I drove south until I ran out of road," recalls Jonathan. And that put him on the funky island in the Florida Keys known for Ernest Hemingway and a lifestyle as colorful as the gingerbread "conch cottages."

Jonathan was the chef at Blackfin Bistro, a highly regarded Key West restaurant, and Megan, a pastry chef, had worked under such luminaries as Richard Leech at Park Avenue Café and James Beard Award–winning pastry chef Nicole Plue. They decided that

Glazed Donuts
420 Eaton Street
Key West, Florida 33040
(305) 294-9142

www.glazeddonutskw.com

Key West needed a modern, sophisticated donut shop like the ones that were emerging in large cities. The Key West clientele ranges from hundreds of sailors on the navy base where President Harry Truman spent time during the winters of his presidency to art gallery owners to tourists—some of whom vacation on the island while thousands more throng ashore for a few hours while their cruise ships are in port.

Glazed Donuts opened on Easter Sunday of 2012, and it's open from 7:00 a.m. to 3:00 p.m. every day. The couple arrives at 4:30 a.m.—"just as the bar crowd is going to sleep," says Megan—and by opening, they've stacked the case with about two-hundred and fifty donuts. They then continue to cook and restock until after noon. Everything is homemade, including the chocolate sprinkles topping the multi-level Chocolate Lover's Donut.

The shop produces both yeast-raised and cake donuts, and it emphasizes vibrant fruit flavors. Of course there is a Key Lime donut, filled with tart custard and topped with toasted meringue and graham cracker crumbs. Other favorites are the piña colada donut topped with candied pineapple and the blood orange bulls-eye with homemade marmalade in the filling.

Edible tropical flowers crown the donuts: there's a purple orchid atop the vanilla orchid brûlée, and mango is joined with hibiscus. Unusual fruits like prickly pear and candied tart kumquats have cycled through the kitchen, and Megan spikes the filling of the maple bacon donut with bourbon and candies the bits of bacon for the top.

The options at Glazed Donuts change seasonally, although Key West is rarely chilly. But in the fall and winter, flavors like pumpkin pecan praline and almond brown butter are options, and Christmas donuts are made from gingerbread and cut into star shapes.

The motto of Glazed Donuts is "everything in moderation, including moderation." So while navy men in uniform might grab a cappuccino or café con leche in the morning, the shop also nabbed a limited liquor license soon after opening. That means that tourists can sip a mimosa with their orange creamsicle donut or enjoy a beer with the Black and Tan on St. Patrick's Day.

GLAZED DONUTS & COFFEE'S PINEAPPLE BRÛLÉE DONUT

Makes 12 to 14

DONUTS

1 batch of Jelly Donuts (page 106), Brioche Donuts (page 95), or Fluffy Yeast-Raised Donuts (page 69) with ½ teaspoon freshly grated nutmeg added to the dough

FROSTING AND GARNISH

½ ripe fresh pineapple

1½ cups granulated sugar, divided

½ vanilla bean

3 to 3½ cups confectioners' sugar

THIS ELEGANT and delicious topping is admittedly a lot of work, but the kudos you'll receive when serving the donuts makes it well worth it. Creating the pineapple slices and glaze is not difficult, so you can simplify considerably by eliminating the final brûlée step.

Prepare the donut recipe, with the additional nutmeg, according to the instructions, up to frying the donuts.

While the dough is rising for the first time, prepare the topping. Preheat the oven to 325°F and line two baking sheets with parchment paper.

Remove all the rind from the pineapple with a sharp serrated knife. Cut the pineapple into ¼-inch-thick slices. Use the same cutter used to cut the donuts to cut out the core and trim the edges of each pineapple slice. Arrange the slices on one of the prepared baking sheets. Discard the core pieces and arrange the trimmed scraps on the other baking sheet. Sprinkle 3 tablespoons of the sugar over the slices, and sprinkle 3 tablespoons of the sugar over the scraps.

Cut the vanilla bean in half lengthwise and use the tip of a small spoon to scrape out the seeds. Add the seeds and scraped vanilla bean to the pan with the scraps.

Bake both pans for 1 hour, stirring the scraps and turning over the slices midway through the baking time. Remove the pineapple slices and scraps from the oven and allow them to cool. Remove and discard the vanilla bean.

While the pineapple is baking, combine ½ cup of the sugar and ½ cup water in a small saucepan, and bring to a boil over medium-high heat, stirring occasionally. Set aside to cool.

Combine the cooled sugar syrup and the pineapple scraps in a blender or food processor fitted with the steel blade and purée. Pour the mixture into a shallow bowl, and whisk in the confectioners' sugar. Press a sheet of plastic wrap directly into the surface to keep the glaze from hardening.

Heat at least 2 inches of oil to a temperature of 375°F in a Dutch oven or deep skillet. Place a few layers of paper towels on a baking sheet and top it with a wire cooling rack. Place a few layers of paper towels on a second baking sheet.

Fry the pineapple slices for 30 to 40 seconds, or until brown. Remove them from the oil and drain them on the rack. Lower the flame under the oil so that the oil temperature drops to 350°F.

Carefully slide a few donuts into the hot oil, being careful not to crowd the pan and making sure that the donuts do not touch each other. Once the donuts float to the top of the oil, fry them for 1 to 1½ minutes per side, or until evenly browned.

Drain the donuts on the rack, blotting them gently with additional paper towels. Fry the remaining donuts and the donut holes in the same manner. While the donuts are still warm, dip the tops into the glaze, turning to coat them well. Place them with the glazed side up on a wire rack set over a sheet of waxed paper. Dip the pineapple slices into the glaze and place them on top of the dipped donuts. Let the donuts stand for 20 minutes, or until the glaze is set.

Sprinkle the remaining granulated sugar on top of the donuts and hold a kitchen torch over them to melt and caramelize the sugar. Serve within a few hours.

The donuts can be fried up to 4 hours in advance. Heat them in a 150°F oven for 3 minutes, or until warm, before glazing and finishing them.

BRÛLÉE WITHOUT THE BOTHER
Certain foods, like *crème brûlée* itself, can be popped under a preheated broiler to caramelize the sugar if you don't have a kitchen torch. But I tried that technique with these donuts and it was a disaster; the donuts were ruined. But here's a sneaky way to get the job done, although it takes a bit longer than a torch. Hold a large metal cooking spoon or solid spatula in the flame of a gas burner or on top of an electric heating element until it is very hot. Then press the hot metal gently onto the sugar and it will caramelize.

RHINO DOUGHNUTS & COFFEE

Most modern donut shops begin with the passion of a pastry chef. But that's not the case with Rhino Doughnuts & Coffee, an emerging boutique chain supplying four shops from a central commissary in south Florida. Here the love of donuts began with the owners, who then hired a pastry chef who shared their passion.

The owners—real estate broker Athan "Tom" Prakas and businessman Davin Tran—had independently decided that their region needed the sort of exciting donuts they had sampled in other cities, and when a mutual friend introduced them, they decided to join forces rather than compete.

Naming the shops "Rhino" was their idea. They believe the innovative flavors of their donuts (along with the muffins and cinnamon rolls sold at the shops) offer a big and bold alternative to the other shops in their region. The image of a rhino was not far off. And while the animal is hardly native to the region, the climate was similar to their habitat. Even the delivery trucks, which have rhino horns mounted on them, conform to the motif.

While Tom and Davin had the vision, it's chef Keith Freiman who makes the reality so delicious. Keith knows this particular market well. After graduating from the Culinary Institute of America in Hyde Park, New York, this native New Yorker moved to Miami and became known as one of the best pastry chefs in the region.

After a few years in the kitchen of noted Florida chef Mark Milatello, he served as pastry chef at the

Miami branch of famed New York steak house Smith & Wollensky for five years and then spent a few years creating indulgent desserts for the Miami branch of Philippe, an upscale Chinese restaurant.

"What I do is try to incorporate aspects of everyone's favorite dessert into donut form," he says, giving some examples: chocolate pudding pie donuts, innovative fillings like blackberry jam with anise-flavored tarragon. Another customer favorite is Nutella banana, with a bit of rum in the glaze.

The colors of Rhino's donuts are as vibrant as their flavors. While they use no artificial coloring or preservatives, Keith's glazes are vivid hues rather than pastels. That also intensifies the flavor of the ingredients.

Rhino does both yeast-raised and cake donuts, as well as an assortment of daily muffins and old-fashioned sticky buns. Some of the flavors—like a guava and cream cheese filling—reflect the geographic location, and Keith works with local farmers to source ingredients whenever possible. All of the doughs, fillings, frostings, and other toppings are made in house by a team of chefs.

While Rhino's shops don't offer the aroma of donuts cooking, the foodstuffs are incredibly fresh. The central kitchen supplying the shops delivers all day long, so customers can still get donuts warm from the fryer.

There are currently four locations.

126 NE 2nd Street
Boca Raton, Florida 33432
(855) RHINO74

8085 West Oakland Boulevard
Sunrise, Florida 33351
(855) RHINO74

300 SW 1st Avenue
Fort Lauderdale, Florida 33301
(855) RHINO74

107 Commercial Boulevard
Lauderdale-by-the-Sea, Florida 33308
(855) RHINO74

www.rhinodoughnuts.com

THE HEAVENLY DONUT COMPANY

★ BIRMINGHAM, ALABAMA ★

While the owners are a young couple, the underlying premise of the Heavenly Donut Company is old-fashioned Southern hospitality. The motto could easily be "come on in and sit a spell."

The bright and cheery shop is far bigger than necessary to sell donuts from the case, and it's open until late at night. There's free Wi-Fi and free coffee refills. Children can have birthday parties, at which they get to decorate their own donuts as well as eating some "birthday donut cake." The owners, Kimberly and Brock Beiersdoerfer, promote local

The Heavenly Donut Company
4911 Cahaba River Road
Birmingham, Alabama 35243
(205) 536-7200

www.theheavenlydonutco.com

artists by allowing them to hang their works for sale on the walls, and their church uses the space for Bible study classes a few times a week.

But it's still all about the donuts—and the fritters. Lots of options built from a number of hand-crafted doughs and fillings. Everything is made in small batches continually during the day.

The yeast donut can be ordered with one of six glazes, and the toppings glued on by the glaze might be crushed Oreo cookies, sprinkles, or maple bacon. The same raised dough forms the exterior of the bismarcks—which have fillings ranging from Bavarian cream to lemon curd and raspberry—and it is also swirled into cinnamon rolls, which can be ordered glazed or frosted with chocolate or caramel.

On the other side of the case are the cake donuts, which are of equal number. They include blueberry, vanilla, sour cream, red velvet, and triple chocolate, and the number of frostings equals that on the yeast-raised side. In addition to the donuts, the South is known for fritters, and the Heavenly Donut Company prepares them with both apples and peaches.

Some people visit the shop on the specific day they know their favorite will be appearing in the case. On Saturday mornings there are old-fashioned New Orleans–style beignets, while strawberry cake donuts are featured on Tuesdays, and key lime custard bismarcks are a Wednesday special. Peanut butter and jelly donuts are on Thursdays, and those wonderful flavors of chocolate and hazelnut are joined on Fridays in a Nutella donut.

Kimberly and Brock both left desk jobs to launch their donut shop. She holds an MBA, and her eleven years of experience in event planning and marketing really gave her a feel for the local community. He shared his wife's dream of owning their own small business and reaching out to the people around them, and he left a career in corporate benefits consulting for companies all around Alabama.

In 2011 the couple contacted a local businessman and asked him to mentor them through the process of launching a small business. His first suggestion was to also be mentored by the owner of a successful donut shop, and they contacted Don DeWeese at Gibson's in Memphis (page 137), who allowed them to train in his kitchen and then sent one of his cooks to Birmingham to help them set up their own kitchen.

The shop opened in 2013, and Brock says it fulfills all their hopes. "It's wonderful to see people come in and after a few minutes they've made what was an ordinary day into a small celebration," he says.

THE TATONUT SHOP

★ OCEAN SPRINGS, MISSISSIPPI ★

While some people may think that adding potato to a donut sounds like a bizarre marriage, they change their minds once they've had a yeast-raised potato donut at the TatoNut Shop. In the wonderful world of food chemistry, the addition of potato to a baked good—or in this case a fried good—cuts back on gluten formation, so the donuts are ethereally light and almost melt in your mouth.

While the TatoNut Shop, housed in an adorable yellow clapboard building with awnings sheltering the outside tables, also makes a full range of cake donuts, ranging from devil's food and blueberry to strawberry and pumpkin, the vast majority of the daily production of three-hundred to four-hundred dozen donuts a day is permutations on the potato dough. The plain glazed donut reigns supreme, but the dough is also braided into twists and turned into what the shop names a Persian, its variation on a cinnamon bun.

You could say that donuts were destiny for Ocean Springs native David Mohler. His father opened a Spudnuts franchise in the Gulf Coast village in 1960 to supplement his income as an air traffic controller, because he had seven sons to feed at home. He would work almost all night making donuts and then head to his day job. After work and a meal, along with a few hours of sleep, it started all over again.

David was in the middle of the pack age-wise, and he remembers going to the shop before he went to school to help with the morning rush. It was in the early 1970s that the name of the shop was changed to the TatoNut, and one of David's brothers

The TatoNut Shop
1114 Government Street
Ocean Springs, Mississippi 39564
(228) 872-2076

www.tatonut.com

ran it for some time while David was working in other parts of the country.

David returned and took over the shop in 1983, when he was 23 years old. It was in the shop that he met his wife, Theresa, who has worked alongside him for the past twenty years. David and Theresa close the shop on Sundays and Mondays every week so they can rest up for the five grueling days they're open.

In addition to the donuts, the shop also sells unusual flavors of coffee beans, including German Chocolate Cake, Cinnamon Butter Cookie, and Irish Cream. It's also known for its delicious fruit smoothies.

Ocean Springs was one of the communities devastated by Hurricane Katrina in 2005. While the shop was not harmed, many of the employees' homes were destroyed. And, of course, the shop's supply lines for ingredients from New Orleans took months to restore. That was when the shop started making bits of fried dough from whatever scraps were left from other donuts. They became known as "Katrina Pieces," and they're still being made today as a reminder of the resilience the town demonstrated during that sad time.

THE RISE AND FALL OF SPUDNUT

When David Mohler's father decided to open a donut shop, he bought a Spudnut franchise, because in 1960 Spudnut was the only truly national donut company. The slogan was "Coast to Coast, from Alaska to Mexico," and with more than 350 outlets selling upwards of 400,000 donuts daily, it was clearly the Dunkin' Donuts and Krispy Kreme of its day.

So what happened? Today there are only a handful of Spudnut Shops in the country, and those are run independently. The business had gone from riches to rags due to some faulty business decisions.

The founders, brothers Al and Bob Pelton, had sampled light and fluffy donuts made with potato in Germany. After their trip, they returned to their homes in Salt Lake City and started experimenting—everything from making donuts with mashed potatoes to making dough with the water in which potatoes were cooked. After discovering that a combination of potato flour with wheat flour produced the desired result, they opened the first Spudnut Shop in 1940.

In 1964 the company developed a process to flash-freeze its dough, replacing the dry mix. The chain even had a mascot, Mr. Spudnut. He looked very much like today's Mr. Peanut from Planters, but as a donut tipping his hat rather than wearing it.

The Pelton brothers sold the company in 1968 to National Oven Products, Inc., based in the state of Washington and owned by Pace Industries, a Canadian firm. Spudnut Shops continued to grow, and then in 1971 Pace Industries sold the company to Dakota Bake-N-Serve. Within a few years they retired Mr. Spudnut, but continued to supply products.

But very soon thereafter the owner of Dakota Bake-N-Serve became involved in a disastrous land deal involving the Sacramento River Delta. The parent company was forced to close in 1979. At that point there were more than 600 stores in the United States, Canada, and Mexico, and an additional 170 outlets in Japan. A decade later there were less than thirty. With the parent company closed there was no longer a source for the dough or the dry mix.

MORE AND MORE PEOPLE ACROSS THE NATION ARE ACCEPTING THE CORDIAL INVITATION TO

Meet Mr. Spudnut

COAST TO COAST..
ALASKA TO MEXICO

SPUDNUTS*
America's Finest Food Confection

Made of the finest ingredients . . . cooked to a rich, golden-brownness in highest quality shortening . . . SPUDNUTS are light as the fluffiest cloud, vitamin packed, quickly digestible, a source of almost instant energy. Morning, noon or night as a whole meal, a dessert, a between-meals snack there's no treat like SPUDNUTS. The whole family loves 'em — they're perfect for parties! More than 250 franchised dealers throughout the nation are ready to serve you.

See 'em made - - buy 'em hot - - and by the sack!
SOLD ONLY IN THE GENUINE MR. SPUDNUT BAG

*What is a SPUDNUT? It's a delightfully different pastry food confection that will bring you a new, remembered eating experience! Buy a dozen at your dealer's today!

Exclusive Spudnut franchises Available. Write FRANCHISE DIVISION, Pelton's Spudnuts, Inc., 1488 South State Street, Salt Lake City, Utah. Canadian Offices: 1207 Burrard, Vancouver, B. C. Spudnuts — A tasty, Pelton pastry product, sold only by authorized, franchised dealers. Copyright 1949

129

POTATO DONUTS

Makes 12

¾ pound russet potatoes, peeled and diced

4 tablespoons (½ stick) unsalted butter, at room temperature

1¾ cups granulated sugar, divided

2 large eggs, at room temperature

½ cup whole milk

½ teaspoon pure vanilla extract

2 teaspoons baking powder

½ teaspoon salt

¼ teaspoon baking soda

2½ cups all-purpose flour, plus more for dusting

Vegetable oil for frying

1 teaspoon ground cinnamon

RIGHT AFTER World War II, potato donuts were all the rage. Dubbed "spudnuts" they were the foundation of a national chain, and independent shops would also have a few in their cases. Potato donuts are light and fluffy, and the secret to keeping them that way is to not work the dough too vigorously once the flour is added.

Cover the potato cubes with salted water and bring to a boil over high heat. Reduce the heat to low and cook the potato cubes for 12 to 15 minutes, or until very tender when pierced with the tip of a paring knife. Drain the potatoes and push them through a potato ricer or mash them until very smooth with a potato masher. Measure out ¾ cup of the mashed potato, and set aside to cool.

Combine the butter and ¾ cup of the sugar in the bowl of a stand mixer fitted with the paddle attachment. Beat at low speed to combine and then increase the speed to medium and beat for 1 minute, or until the mixture comes together. Add the eggs, one at a time, and beat until the mixture is light and fluffy, scraping the sides of the bowl as necessary. Add the mashed potatoes, milk, vanilla, baking powder, salt, and baking soda, and beat well.

Add the flour and beat at low speed until thoroughly combined. Grease a large sheet of plastic wrap and scrape the dough into the center. Make the dough into a round pancake about 1 inch thick. Refrigerate the dough for at least 1 hour, or up to 24 hours.

Dust a surface and rolling pin with flour. Roll the chilled dough to a thickness of ½ inch. Use a donut cutter dipped in flour to cut out as many donuts as possible; alternatively, use a 2½-inch cookie cutter and then cut out holes with a ½-inch cutter. Transfer the donuts and holes carefully to a baking sheet sprinkled with flour. Reroll the scraps one time to a thickness of ½ inch and cut out more

(recipe continues)

donuts and holes. Allow the donuts to sit for 10 minutes to dry the exteriors slightly.

Heat at least 2 inches of oil to a temperature of 365°F in a Dutch oven or deep skillet. Place a few layers of paper towels on a baking sheet and top it with a wire cooling rack.

Carefully slide a few donuts into the hot oil, being careful not to crowd the pan and making sure that the donuts do not touch each other. Fry the donuts for 2 minutes per side, or until evenly browned.

Drain the donuts on the rack, blotting them gently with additional paper towels. Fry the remaining donuts and the donut holes in the same manner.

Mix the remaining sugar and the cinnamon in a shallow bowl. Once the donuts are cool enough to handle, coat them in the bowl of cinnamon sugar. Serve as soon as possible.

The dough can be refrigerated for up to 2 days, and the cut-out donuts can be refrigerated for up to 1 day. It is best to not fry the donuts until just prior to serving.

If your dough is soft and the rings lose their shape when you transfer them to the hot oil, transfer them on a metal spatula that has been heavily greased with vegetable oil.

CAFÉ DU MONDE

While there are now seven outposts around the region, when natives and tourists alike say "Café du Monde," what they visualize is the old beige stucco building with the green-and-white-striped awnings in the French Quarter of New Orleans, across from Jackson Park and in the shadow of the cathedral. Café au lait and beignets thickly encrusted with confectioners' sugar have been served on this site since 1862.

This location is open 24/7 except for Christmas Day and when the occasional hurricane comes too close. Its reopening following Hurricane Katrina in 2005 made the national news.

Café du Monde
800 Decatur Street
New Orleans, Louisiana 70116
(504) 525-4544

www.cafedumonde.com

The café au lait is quite warm because the milk added to it is heated, and it's somewhat bitter because it's laced with chicory. But that bitterness dissipates immediately as soon as you bite into a beignet. These puffy squares of fried dough are always served in piping-hot orders of three, and they are rich and tender as well as delicious. Relatively new to the menu are some cold drinks, including iced café au lait, which is a welcome treat in the heat of New Orleans most of the year.

French colonists brought beignets to Louisiana in the eighteenth century, and they quickly became part of classic Creole cooking. In France beignets are made from pâte à choux, the dough used to make cream puffs and French crullers (page 24). But the New Orleans version popularized at Café du Monde uses yeast dough that has shortening added to cut the gluten and help them to puff when fried.

There's a drill to successfully get a table at Café du Monde, which has lines at any time of the day or night. If you're near the front of the line and see people looking like they're finishing their snack—dabbing their mouths or brushing off their clothes—start walking to the table. It's seat yourself, and it's not an orderly first-come, first-served. It's more a matter of being in the right place at the right time, because bodies will fill the chairs just as soon as they are empty.

Café du Monde is known for quick—but somewhat surly—service. If you're not in a server's group of tables, he'll tell you, and point in the direction of someone else. But quick service means that the tables turn over really fast, so don't be put off by a long line. Also remember that this is not a place to wear dark-colored clothing. Go for something that won't show the confectioners' sugar that everyone carries away like a souvenir.

CALAS CAKES ARE ALSO PART OF CREOLE TRADITION

At the time Café du Monde opened in 1862, beignets were not the only fried treats enjoyed in the French Quarter. Across Jackson Square, churchgoers leaving St. Louis Cathedral were greeted by African-American women, many wearing bandanas, selling hot rice fritters from baskets on their heads with the cry of *"Calas, belles, calas, tout chaud!"* which translates to "beautiful *calas,* very hot."

The Old Coffeepot Restaurant
714 St. Peter Street
New Orleans, Louisiana 70116
(504) 524-3500

www.theoldcoffeepot.com

The fritters were made from leftover rice mixed into a sweetened egg batter, and they're frequently dusted with confectioners' sugar after frying. *Calas* probably arrived with slaves from the parts of Africa where rice was grown, and during the first half of the eighteenth century, when the city was under French rule, slaves were given one day off a week, which was usually a Sunday. *Calas* were a treat made in the house and shared with friends and family.

The selling of *calas* took on a vital role in the late 1700s, when Louisiana was under Spanish rule and slaves could purchase their freedom under an act called *coartación,* which more than fourteen hundred did. Much of the money for their freedom came from selling *calas* on their one day off.

The Louisiana Purchase in 1803 reversed the liberal Spanish policy, but *calas* vendors remained plentiful in New Orleans well into the twentieth century. They're still on the menu at the Old Coffeepot Restaurant, a landmark in the French Quarter that opened in 1894, and they're served at breakfast, lunch, and dinner.

BEIGNETS

Makes 24

1 tablespoon active
dry yeast

⅓ cup granulated sugar,
divided

1 cup water, heated
to 110°F to 115°F

2 large eggs, at room
temperature

2 tablespoons unsalted butter,
melted and cooled

3 cups all-purpose flour,
plus more for dusting

½ teaspoon salt

Vegetable oil for frying

Confectioners' sugar
for dusting

PART OF THE "MAGIC" of beignets as they're served at Café du Monde is that they're crisp but also airy, and that they're puffed up. The puffing is created by steam; the dough is very wet. That moisture makes it difficult to roll, which is why the rising takes place in the refrigerator. You'll also need to use a lot of flour on your rolling pin and surface. But serving these hot with a thick dusting of confectioners' sugar is well worth the trouble.

Combine the yeast, 2 tablespoons of the sugar, and water in the bowl of a stand mixer fitted with the paddle attachment, and mix well. Set aside for about 10 minutes while the yeast proofs.

When the yeast looks frothy, add the eggs and butter and mix well. Add the remaining sugar, flour, and salt, and beat at low speed until the flour is incorporated to form a soft dough. Beat the dough at medium speed for 2 minutes.

Lightly grease the inside of a large mixing bowl with softened butter or vegetable oil. Add the dough, turning it so it is lightly greased all over. Cover the bowl loosely with a sheet of oiled plastic wrap or a damp tea towel, and refrigerate it for at least 4 hours, or until it has doubled in bulk, or up to 24 hours.

Heat at least 2 inches of oil to a temperature of 350°F in a Dutch oven or deep skillet. Dust a surface, baking sheet, and rolling pin heavily with flour. Line another baking sheet with a few layers of paper towels and set a wire cooling rack inside of it.

Punch the dough down and divide it in half. Roll the first half into a rectangle ¼ inch thick. Using a pizza wheel, cut the dough into 2½- to 3-inch squares, and transfer the squares to the floured baking sheet. Repeat with the second half of the dough.

Carefully slide a few beignets into the hot oil, being careful not to crowd the pan and making sure that they do not touch each other. Once the beignets float to the top of the oil, fry them for 1 to 1½ minutes per side, or until evenly browned.

Drain the beignets on the rack, blotting them very gently with additional paper towels. Fry the remaining beignets in the same manner. While the beignets are still hot, dust them heavily with confectioners' sugar and serve immediately.

The dough can be refrigerated for up to 1 day. But the beignets should not be rolled or fried until just prior to serving.

FOX'S DONUT DEN

Fox's Donut Den is an icon for more than its legendary donuts. Preserving its antique neon sign with the image of a young Dutch boy became a *cause célèbre* in its Green Hills neighborhood of the Music City in 2009.

But first the donuts: In 1973 Norm Fox, a graduate of Lipscomb University who was studying for an advanced degree in biology, purchased part of a franchise in Nashville from Memphis-based Harlow's Honey Fluff Doughnuts. It was then that the bakery first launched its reputation for yeast-raised rings and apple fritters. Four years later, Norm moved the business to its present location, bought the now-famous sign from Harlow's, and had it installed at his shop that—at the suggestion of his wife—became Fox's Donut Den.

The shop is open from early morning until midnight, although Norm resisted staying open all night. Customers flock to the variety of donuts— even the donut holes have their own fans. Many reviewers stress that getting a sack of blueberry cake donut holes or the devil's food cake donuts requires arriving early.

Fox's Donut Den
3900 Hillsboro Pike
Nashville, Tennessee 37215
(615) 385-1021

www.foxsdonutden.com

The options are now expanded to include bagels and muffins for those who may be a bit more health-conscious, but Norm says that the majority of the business has never been anything but donuts and fritters. In addition to the many sweet options, Fox's also sells savory sausage rolls and kolaches early in the day as breakfast options.

And all of these treats can be found in the shop behind the newly restored quirky neon sign. In 2009 Brookside Properties, the owner of the strip mall in which Fox's is located, required all tenants to update their signage to conform to a uniform, modern look. But customers balked at the static piece of painted fiberglass, and after a few months the Dutch boy and his dancing letters were restored.

GIBSON'S DONUTS

★ **MEMPHIS, TENNESSEE** ★

If you have a hankering for a donut at any time of the day or night in Memphis, Gibson's Donuts is the place to go. This shop near the University of Memphis, founded by Lowell Gibson in 1967, is open around the clock every day of the week. It's known as a northern outpost of the buttermilk drop donut that is native to New Orleans, as well as for options ranging from French crullers and red velvet donuts crowned with cream cheese frosting to maple bacon donuts and bumpy apple fritters.

The cooks come in to start making donuts for the next day at 10:00 p.m., so by 11:00 p.m. some of those are ready for shelving in the case. That's when the fun starts. Every night there's a donut sale for eager college students who arrive for the event. At that point, six donuts can be purchased for $1.40. It doesn't take more than a few minutes to clean out the case.

Don DeWeese purchased the shop from Gibson in 1996, and after a few years of his son Blair running the shop, it's now being managed by his younger son, Britton. Britton remembers eating the buttermilk drops when visiting his grandmother in the French Quarter.

The buttermilk drop donut was a specialty at McKenzie's Bakery in New Orleans. McKenzie's closed for a few years, and while it has subsequently reopened, it is no longer run by the family that founded it. Don DeWeese worked with the owner to learn the all-important method. Buttermilk drop

Gibson's Donuts
760 Mt. Moriah Road
Memphis, Tennessee 38117
(901) 682-8200

donuts do not have a hole in the center; they have an indentation that looks like the stem end of a peach. He learned the secret of achieving that look and at what temperature to fry the donuts in the Big Easy. Along with glazed donuts, buttermilk drops are on the menu every day, and the *Memphis Commercial Appeal* listed them as "one of the 100 foods to eat in Memphis before you die."

Gibson's produces thousands of donuts a day; the record was 12,000 on a single day. While the donuts are all fried at the shop, the mix that creates them is purchased from a bakery supplier. But the creativity of the flavors and presentation is all Gibson's. Britton DeWeese creates a "Donut of the Month" each month; some of the customers' favorites are strawberry cake and key lime pie.

Gibson's also embellishes a long éclair-shaped donut with the city's area code, 901. The frosting is very high, and the inspiration came from Justin Timberlake, who lives in Memphis and uses the numerals as the name of his brand of vodka. The secret to some of the fruit glazes' vivid colors is Kool-Aid mix, an important technique when replicating the royal blue and white of the shop's beloved University of Memphis Tigers.

BUTTERMILK DROPS

Makes 16 to 18

2⅔ cups all-purpose flour

1½ cups granulated sugar, divided

1½ teaspoons baking powder

½ teaspoon baking soda

½ teaspoon salt

½ teaspoon freshly grated nutmeg

1 large egg, at room temperature

1 large egg yolk, at room temperature

1 cup buttermilk

3 tablespoons unsalted butter, melted and cooled

1 teaspoon ground cinnamon

Vegetable oil for frying

IN THE NEW ORLEANS tradition, the buttermilk drops at Gibson's are coated in cinnamon sugar. These are one of the easiest types of donuts to make because the dough is literally dropped by the spoonful into the hot oil.

Combine the flour, ½ cup of the sugar, baking powder, baking soda, salt, and nutmeg in a large mixing bowl. Whisk well to mix the ingredients. Combine the egg and egg yolk in a mixing bowl and whisk well. Stir in the buttermilk and melted butter, and whisk well.

Pour the wet ingredients into the dry ingredients and stir with a wooden spoon until the mixture comes together and only small lumps remain. Do not beat the batter until smooth.

Combine the remaining sugar with the cinnamon in a shallow bowl.

Heat at least 2 inches of oil to a temperature of 375°F in a Dutch oven or deep skillet. Place a few layers of paper towels on a baking sheet and top it with a wire cooling rack.

Drop balls of dough about the size of a walnut into the hot oil, being careful not to crowd the pan. Fry the balls for 1½ to 2 minutes per side, turning them gently with a wire mesh spoon.

Drain the drops on the rack, blotting them gently with additional paper towels. Fry the remaining dough in the same manner. Roll the drops in the cinnamon sugar, and serve immediately.

The dough can be refrigerated for up to 3 hours. Fry the buttermilk drops just prior to serving.

VARIATIONS: **Add 1 cup of fresh blueberries or raspberries, sliced strawberries, or diced cherries or peaches to the dough.**

MINNESOTA

WISCONSIN

10

9

MICH.

4

5 · 6 · 7 · 8

2

IOWA

OHIO

3

IND.

1

ILLINOIS

KANSAS

11

Chapter 4

THE MIDWESTERN STATES

There's no shortage of traditional or modern donuts here in the nation's heartland. The largest groups of immigrants to this region were from Germany, Central Europe, and the Scandinavian countries, and all of these people held donuts dear to their hearts.

Finding nouvelle donuts is where the big cities such as Chicago and Minneapolis enter the picture, but smaller cities are also on the cusp of crullers. In Cleveland, a baker couple is building a donut business that incorporates the products of the city's emerging coterie of artisan micro-breweries, and in Wichita, a donut shop is serving as a catalyst to one neighborhood's development into an arts center.

HOLTMAN'S DONUTS

Decades ago, when other urban areas were being denuded of historic architecture in the name of urban renewal, a large section of Cincinnati was spared the wrecking ball. Now the Over-the-Rhine section (abbreviated OTR) is the "Brooklyn of the Midwest," full of exciting shops and restaurants in Italianate and Gothic Revival buildings. And that's where you'll find the newest location of Holtman's Donuts, now being run by the third generation of the family.

Danny Plazarin and his wife, Katie Willing, opened the OTR shop in 2013, buoyed by the choice of Holtman's at their other locations as the "Best Donuts" by *Cincinnati Magazine* the year before. Their donuts, made a few times a day, share the traditional recipes that led to that accolade. It took them two years to find a space they knew would work for their third location, and Katie had never been a baker before immersing herself at Holtman's.

Charles Holtman opened his first shop in nearby Clermont County, to the east of Cincinnati, in 1960. At one point he owned a baker's dozen of shops, but by the time he turned the business over to his daughter and son-in-law, Toni and Chuck Plazarin, there were two shops to run, one in Loveland and the other in nearby Williamsburg.

Customers at the OTR shop know they're approaching Holtman's both by the bright pink sign—a nibbled donut with sprinkles—projecting out from the nineteenth-century storefront and from the aroma (all three shops make donuts continually all day). The city location also has a picture window, so standing on line becomes a spectator sport.

The shops feature a wide range of yeast-raised and cake donuts. Maple bacon, with the bacon applied like tiny squares of mosaic tile to the frosting, is now the most popular donut, but also cherished are the twisted cinnamon glazed donuts, as well as flavors ranging from a chocolate-iced donut topped with chopped peanuts to a blueberry cake donut with vanilla icing.

In addition to rotating frostings and fillings, Holtman's also has seasonal specialties. The shops feature lemon cake donuts in the spring, pumpkin in the fall, and red velvet—topped with a luscious cream cheese frosting—in the winter. Locals wait for the black raspberry jelly filling to appear in late summer, and apple fritters are a fall necessity in this orchard-laden part of the country. "While our recipes are still the same quality that they've always had, with no preservatives or box mixes, we are always coming up with new ideas and trying them as specials," says Katie. "That's what makes this job so much fun."

Two new introductions are the popular German chocolate cake donut, which reflects the area's Teutonic heritage, and the true indulgence—the Muddy Pig. It's a chocolate bacon donut that Katie says is "almost addictive" once sampled.

1332 Vine Street
Cincinnati, Ohio 45202
(513) 381-0903

1399 Ohio Route 28
Loveland, Ohio 45140
(513) 575-1077

214 West Main Street
Williamsburg, Ohio 45176
(513) 724-3865

www.holtmansdonutshop.com

GERMAN CHOCOLATE DONUTS

Makes 12

1 batch Chocolate Cake Donuts (page 174)

1 cup chopped pecans

1 cup evaporated milk

¾ cup granulated sugar

6 tablespoons (¾ stick) unsalted butter, sliced

2 large egg yolks, beaten

½ teaspoon pure vanilla extract

1 cup firmly packed sweetened coconut flakes

MOST PEOPLE order German chocolate anything because of the yummy frosting, thick with crunchy pecans and sweet coconut. This donut version makes it portable for picnics, too.

Make and fry the donuts as specified in the recipe. Preheat the oven to 350°F. Toast the pecans in the oven for 5 to 7 minutes, or until browned. Remove the nuts from the oven and set aside.

Combine the milk, sugar, butter, egg yolks, and vanilla in a saucepan. Bring to a boil over medium heat, whisking constantly. Reduce the heat to low and simmer the mixture for 10 minutes, or until thickened, stirring constantly. Stir in the pecans and coconut, and allow the frosting to cool to room temperature before spreading a thick layer on the donuts. Serve immediately.

The donuts can be fried and frozen for up to 2 weeks before topping them with the frosting. Allow them to thaw at room temperature, and then reheat them in a 150°F oven for 3 minutes.

GERMAN CHOCOLATE HAS NO TIE TO GERMANY

While the parentage of the Sacher torte can be traced to the legendary hotel in Vienna, German chocolate cake, and its donut variation, did not originate in Germany. In 1852, an American named Sam German developed a type of dark baking chocolate for the Baker's Chocolate Company. In his honor, they named the product Baker's German's Dark Chocolate. More than a century later, in 1957, a recipe for German's Chocolate Cake appeared in a newspaper, and General Foods, which owned Baker's Chocolate at the time, distributed the recipe nationally, thus significantly boosting sales of its product. In subsequent versions of the recipe the possessive form was lost, and German's chocolate cake morphed into German chocolate cake.

BREWNUTS

All donut recipes call for some sort of liquid, and if the liquid in everything destined for the fryer is small-batch craft beer, what you have is a Brewnut. Some Brewnuts are cake or old-fashioned sour cream donuts, while others are yeast-raised, and all the various whimsically named flavors are the brainchildren of owners Shelley Fasulko and John Pippin.

As well as loving each other, the engaged couple both love food and beer. It was Shelley, who was working as a clinical researcher in a hospital while John was in accounting and finance, who came up with the concept of merging the two. "Cleveland is still a Rust Belt city at heart," says Shelley, "and what could be more iconic Americana than merging beer and donuts!"

The two started experimenting in their home kitchen in the fall of 2013, and soon after had perfected some recipes. They rented space in the Cleveland Culinary Launch & Kitchen, home to many small food businesses, and started selling Brewnuts not only to coffee shops but also to bars by the end of 2013.

Very soon their customers had favorites among the offerings. The basic glazed yeast donut is named the Bernie, in honor of legendary Cleveland Browns quarterback Bernie Kosar. It's made with Dortmunder Lager from the Great Lakes Brewing Company, which Shelley describes as the "flagship of the local craft beer movement." While the donut remains the same, Shelley and John change the

Brewnuts
2406 Professor Avenue
Cleveland, Ohio 44113
(216) 744-5424

www.brewnutscle.com

tint in the glaze and add whimsical decorations to keep it visually exciting.

The two also mix it up with their most popular chocolate donut, the Dub Choc, made with Hoppin' Frog Brewery's B.O.R.I.S (Bodacious Oatmeal Russian Imperial Stout). The donut's been topped with everything from candies to dulce de leche with *fleur de sel* on different occasions.

Brewnuts' version of the maple bacon donut is called the Boss Hog. It's made with nut brown ale fermented in whiskey barrels by Elevator Brewing Company that is reduced and combined with organic Ohio maple syrup. Another favorite is the Bumbler, made with Fat Head Brewery's Bumble Berry Blueberry Ale. The Orangina is made with Buffalo Bill's Orange Blossom Cream Ale and topped with chopped pistachio nuts.

The leap to the brick-and-mortar space, which opened in May 2014, was winning a contest. It wasn't the lottery. The Tremont Storefront Incubator Project, a business organization, selected Shelley and John's proposal from more than three dozen entries.

The prize was a storefront location that was rent-free for three months of a ten-month lease and far below market rent for the remainder. The criteria for winning included having a clear business plan for after the incubation period was over and being ready for growth.

Shelley and John made the space as whimsical as their products. There's a Magic Eight ball next to the cash register, faux animal heads deck the walls, and the tip jar is labeled "beer money."

"Brewnuts is a tremendous idea and concept, using craft beer and that whole scene and turning it into something everyone loves—donuts," says Cory Riordan, director of the company that sponsored the contest. "They brought in samples and maybe that's what won the day. You feed me a donut and you get high marks."

Shelley and John still make their donuts—which sometimes sell out within an hour—at the co-op kitchen. They're pondering the next step, and considering a permanent store against options like a food truck or a stall at the local farmers' market. If it ends up a store, they intend to apply for a liquor license so they can sell glasses of the beer alongside the donuts made from them.

CHOCOLATE STOUT DONUTS

Makes 12

DONUTS

1½ cups all-purpose flour, plus more for dusting

½ cup cake flour

½ cup granulated sugar

⅓ cup unsweetened cocoa powder

1½ teaspoons baking powder

½ teaspoon baking soda

½ teaspoon salt

1 large egg, at room temperature

3 tablespoons unsalted butter, melted and cooled

½ cup dark stout beer, such as Guinness

Vegetable oil for frying

GLAZE

1¾ cups confectioners' sugar

¼ cup unsweetened cocoa powder

3 tablespoons dark stout beer, such as Guinness

1 tablespoon light corn syrup

1 teaspoon pure vanilla extract

For the donuts, combine the all-purpose flour, cake flour, sugar, cocoa powder, baking powder, baking soda, and salt in a large bowl and whisk well. Combine the egg, butter, and beer in another mixing bowl, and whisk well.

Add the wet ingredients to the dry ingredients, and whisk until the mixture is just combined. Allow the dough to rest for 10 minutes.

While the dough rests, make the glaze. Combine the confectioners' sugar and cocoa powder in a shallow bowl and whisk well. Add the beer, corn syrup, and vanilla, and whisk until smooth. Press a sheet of plastic wrap directly into the surface of the glaze to keep it from hardening.

Heat at least 2 inches of oil to a temperature of 360°F in a Dutch oven or deep skillet. Place a few layers of paper towels on a baking sheet and top it with a wire cooling rack.

While the oil heats, dust a surface and rolling pin generously with flour. Roll the dough to a thickness of ½ inch. Use a donut cutter dipped in flour to cut out as many donuts as possible; alternatively, use a 2½-inch cookie cutter and then cut out holes with a ½-inch cutter. Transfer the donuts and holes carefully to a baking sheet sprinkled with flour. Reroll the scraps one time to a thickness of ½ inch and cut out more donuts and holes.

Carefully slide a few donuts into the hot oil, being careful not to crowd the pan and making sure that the donuts do not touch each other. Once the donuts float to the top of the oil, fry them for 1 to 1½ minutes per side, or until evenly browned.

(recipe continues)

Drain the donuts on the rack, blotting them gently with additional paper towels. Fry the remaining donuts and the donut holes in the same manner. While the donuts are still warm, dip the tops into the glaze, turning to coat them well. Place them with the glazed side up on a wire rack set over a sheet of waxed paper. Let the donuts stand for 20 minutes, or until the glaze is set.

The donuts can be cut out and refrigerated for up to 1 day, lightly covered with plastic wrap. They should not be fried or glazed more than 6 hours prior to serving.

THE LITTLE DONUT SHOP

Everything about the Little Donut Shop is small—except the flavor of the donuts and the creative way they are elaborately decorated. The shop itself is only about 600 square feet, and it can seat only about a dozen people at a time. The donuts themselves are only about three inches across, but they sell for the small price of one dollar each or a dozen for eight dollars. That means customers can sample many options from the daily rotation of fifteen donuts and really immerse themselves in the donut experience.

The shop, which opened in September 2013, is located right across from the campus of Ohio State University. John Massimiani and John Kastelic, who own the Big Bar & Grill directly above the donut shop, had the space available and thought that the university community would be receptive to creative donuts, although such classics as a vanilla-glazed, cinnamon and sugar, and confectioners' sugar are always available.

The Little Donut Shop produces only vanilla cake donuts as the base for their experimentations. "We consider it like a blank canvas," says Greg Gould, who is the culinary consultant to both the donut shop and restaurant upstairs. And once the donuts are out of the fryer, the chefs begin creating their art.

Of course, there are such classics as crushed M&M's on top of chocolate frosting and almost a whole rasher of chopped bacon encrusting the maple bacon. Of course there is a donut with sprinkles and—of course—they're red and gray. After all, those are the colors of the Ohio State Buckeyes.

The Little Donut Shop
1716 North High Street
Columbus, Ohio 43201
(614) 725-4940

www.littledonut.com

But then there are the more unusual options, like the Dirty Worm. The "dirt" is crushed Oreo cookies and the "worm" is a gummy worm affixed to the top. Another unusual presentation is the Chocolate Pretzel. Two pretzel sticks are arranged like a pair of chopsticks atop chocolate frosting and then sprinkled with sea salt and a chocolate drizzle.

Texture is important in the presentation of the donuts. The Samoa—a donut version of the iconic Girl Scout cookie—is topped with a thick layer of toasted coconut over the chocolate frosting, and then there's more chocolate drizzled in lines across the top. The donut version of strawberry shortcake uses crumbled streusel over strawberry frosting to replicate the sensation of eating crunchy shortcake and is then topped with a deep red strawberry drizzle.

The donuts are made throughout the day, and at closing time, whatever remains in the case is transported upstairs and given away in the Big Bar & Grill. "You can imagine how happy people are to see the bowls of popcorn replaced with trays of donuts," says Greg.

ZINGERMAN'S ROADHOUSE

★ ANN ARBOR, MICHIGAN ★

Zingerman's Roadhouse is a shrine to the wonders of real American food made at home, so of course it's famous for a donut, which can be purchased from a silver trailer parked alongside the restaurant or enjoyed in a donut sundae as dessert.

Noted restaurateur Ari Weinzweig opened this restaurant, on the outskirts of this city near Detroit and home to the University of Michigan, in 2003. That's more than twenty years after he started Zingerman's Deli near the college campus. Alex Young, who has been chef since the Roadhouse's inception, and who won the James Beard Award for Best Chef in the Great Lakes Region in 2012, developed an old-fashioned Dutch donut scented with nutmeg and rich with molasses.

While they are delicious just dusted with muscovado sugar, they are transformed into true decadence when topped with various ice creams and sauces. There is a sundae for each day of the week. The tuesdae on Tuesday, for example, is Dulce Donut with dulce de leche sauce, dulce de leche gelato, whipped cream, and Virginia peanuts; Sunday features the original sundae concept with bourbon-caramel sauce topping vanilla gelato and whipped cream. And Zingerman's does the maple bacon donut craze one better on Mondays, when it serves the Everything Is Better with Bacon Sundae, featuring bacon chocolate gravy, applewood-smoked bacon, vanilla gelato, bourbon-caramel sauce, whipped cream, and peanuts. All sundaes, of

Zingerman's Roadhouse
2501 Jackson Avenue
Ann Arbor, Michigan 48103
(734) 663-3663

www.zingermansroadhouse.com

course, are topped with a bright red cherry, and the gelati come from Zingerman's Creamery, a sister business to the Roadhouse.

But the food preceding the donut at Zingerman's Roadhouse is more than worth your time—as long as you save room for a sundae. What's difficult about the Zingerman's Roadhouse menu is the number of delicious choices, so go with a large group if possible.

The restaurant serves breakfast, lunch, and dinner, and the ingredients for all the dishes are culled from the finest suppliers in the nation.

Some of the highlights are the pit-smoked meats—ranging from pork ribs sourced from famed Niman Ranch to local Amish chickens and pork that is smoked whole for fourteen hours and then hand-shredded. The kitchen makes about six different regional barbecue sauces, all authentic and all delicious. You'll also find the Roadhouse Macaroni & Cheese, chosen by the Food Network as the best in the country. What makes it so special is that it's cooked in a hot skillet so some of the cheese caramelizes. If you'd like to try the recipe, check out my book *Mac & Cheese* (Running Press, 2012).

Weekend brunches are extremely popular, and in case you're not going to be around on Monday for the bacon sundae, the same gravy is served on top of biscuits in the morning.

But always save room for a donut sundae, regardless of what comes first.

ZINGERMAN'S MOLASSES CAKE DONUTS

Makes 18

2½ cups all-purpose flour, plus more for dusting

1½ teaspoons baking powder

1 teaspoon freshly grated nutmeg

¼ teaspoon salt

¼ cup buttermilk, at room temperature

1 large egg, at room temperature

1 large egg yolk, at room temperature

⅓ cup granulated sugar

4 tablespoons (½ stick) unsalted butter, melted and cooled

3 tablespoons molasses

½ teaspoon grated lemon zest

Vegetable oil for frying

⅔ cup muscovado sugar

Sift the flour, baking powder, nutmeg, and salt together in a large mixing bowl. In another mixing bowl, combine the buttermilk, egg, egg yolk, granulated sugar, melted butter, molasses, and lemon zest, and whisk until smooth.

Pour the liquid ingredients into the dry ingredients and stir until just combined. This can also be done in a stand mixer fitted with the paddle attachment at low speed. Scrape the dough into the center of a large sheet of floured plastic wrap and pat it into a pancake about 1 inch thick. Refrigerate the dough for at least 1 hour.

Heat at least 2 inches of oil to a temperature of 360°F in a Dutch oven or deep skillet. Place a few layers of paper towels on a baking sheet and top it with a wire cooling rack.

While the oil heats, dust a surface and rolling pin with flour. Knead the dough gently with greased hands for 1 minute.

Roll the chilled dough to a thickness of ½ inch. Use a 3½-inch donut cutter dipped in flour to cut out as many donuts as possible; alternatively, use a 3½-inch cookie cutter and then cut out holes with a 1-inch cutter. Transfer the donuts and holes carefully to a baking sheet sprinkled with flour. Reroll the scraps one time to a thickness of ½ inch and cut out more donuts and holes.

Carefully slide a few donuts into the hot oil, being careful not to crowd the pan and making sure that the donuts do not touch each other. Once the donuts float to the top of the oil, fry them for 1½ minutes. Gently flip them over with a mesh spoon or long chopstick and fry for 1½ minutes, or until evenly browned.

Drain the donuts on the rack, blotting them gently with additional paper towels. Sprinkle the donuts immediately with the muscovado sugar. Fry the remaining donuts and the donut holes in the same manner. Serve warm.

The dough can be refrigerated for up to 1 day, and the donuts can be refrigerated once rolled and cut out for up to 1 day. Do not fry them until just prior to serving.

Muscovado sugar, sometimes sold as Barbados sugar or moist sugar, has a deep brown color similar to black coffee and a strong taste of molasses. It's now easy to find it, but in a pinch you can substitute dark brown sugar.

THE DOUGHNUT VAULT

The selections are few in number, and the space is so small that if there are more than four people in line they're queuing up on the sidewalk. There are no tables or chairs, although there are crystal chandeliers and robin's-egg-blue walls enlivening the spartan space.

But none of those things have stopped the Doughnut Vault, which opened in 2012, from becoming a foodie mecca. In fact, night owls who frequently close down nearby hipster bars stay awake another few hours for the 8:00 a.m. opening time. While the ostensible closing time is 2:00 p.m., they know that it's really at whatever time the production of the day sells out, which can be by noon or even before.

The menu is fairly set, so there are few choices to make at the front of the line. The super-sized yeast-raised donuts are glazed with vanilla, chocolate, or chestnut. The two cake dough options are a crispy-ridged old-fashioned donut and a trio of thin gingerbread donuts dusted with cinnamon sugar.

No baristas are needed either. There is just one size of coffee and it sells for one dollar.

Beyond the stalwarts on the menu, there is one special donut each day. It could be Birthday Cake (a cake donut with multicolored jimmies on top of the vanilla glaze), or an apple fritter, or a pineapple upside-down cake donut. Green tea, white chocolate, and strawberry have each been cycled into the old-fashioned donut dough, and sometimes addi-

The Doughnut Vault
401½ North Franklin Street
Chicago, Illinois 60654
No phone or email at the shop

www.thedoughnutvault.tumblr.com

tions like pink peppercorns in the glaze give the old-fashioned experience a contemporary twist.

Avid fans consult Tumblr and Twitter not only to check the special flavors of the day, but also to located the Doughnut Vault's van, which was put into service in 2013. The van dates from 1957, and it has a history both as an Air Force vehicle and as a mail truck before its current incarnation as a rolling source of delicious donuts.

The Doughnut Vault is one of the ventures launched by culinary wunderkind Brendan Sodikoff, a trained chef with experience at Thomas Keller's Per Se as well as at Alain Ducasse in New York. But the person he credits as his mentor is Rich Melman, the legendary restaurateur who founded Lettuce Entertain You Enterprises in 1971.

Brendan's concepts, like his mentor's, run the gamut from barbecue joints like Green Street Smoked Meats to High Five Ramen, serving Japanese noodles, and Bavette's Bar and Boeuf, a steakhouse. The Doughnut Vault is located around the corner from Gilt Bar, one of his first ventures. The concept for the donut shop was to use this tiny unused space "as something nice for the community," Brendan says, adding that he never expected it to become a citywide, let alone a national destination.

"I like classic things in pastry, cocktails, and even clothing," he says. "What I care about is investing in traditional products and making them the best."

Brendan's uncommon portfolio of businesses carries over into his ethic. His firm, Hogsalt Hos-pitality, doesn't have a central office. He has an assistant and takes his business meetings at one of his restaurants. But you'll rarely find him at the Doughnut Vault. It's too small and there are no tables.

WAFFLES CAFÉ

CHICAGO, ILLINOIS

The of-the-moment donut trend is hybridizing them with another baked good. It started in 2013 with the much-heralded marriage of a donut and a croissant in New York. Soon after that, Alex Hernandez, the owner of Waffles Café in Chicago, invented the Wonut.

This cross between a donut and a waffle was somewhat popular when he added it to the menu at his first breakfast and lunch spot (opened in 2012), but it became a phenomenon in the spring of 2014 with the opening of his second restaurant.

What happened? The Wonut was the topic of a long posting on the Thrillist website that went viral. A few months later, an Internet search for the word "Wonut" found more than 92,000 references. "We went from making a few dozen a day to order to pumping out upwards of six hundred or more per day," Alex says.

Hernandez had been the manager of upscale restaurants before buying Waffles Café, but he decided he should really learn the culinary side of

203 East Ohio Street
Chicago, Illinois 60611
(312) 846-1242

3611 North Broadway
Chicago, Illinois 60613
(773) 281-8440

www.wafflescafechicago.com

the business before going off on his own. He attended Le Cordon Bleu, and it was his training there that led him to become "Father of the Wonut."

Wonuts are made with a two-step cooking process, and in that way they're similar to bagels. But while a bagel is boiled and then baked, a Wonut is partially cooked in a waffle iron before being fried. Like the waffle batters on which they're based, Wonuts can be yeast-raised, cake, or old-fashioned. Within the world of cake, Wonuts are vanilla, chocolate, and red velvet varieties.

"The batter for Wonuts is thicker than waffle batter because it has to stand up to being fried and then glazed," says Alex, adding that it can't contain too much bulk or the resulting product would be dry. The batter is cooked to the point of solidity on the waffle iron, and then it finishes cooking and gets its crusty exterior in the oil.

The most popular Wonuts to date are the Mexican Chocolate, which starts with a chocolate cake batter and is topped with candied orange peel and chocolate ganache, and the Birthday Wonut, which is a delicately flavored yeast-raised item smothered in royal icing and colored sprinkles.

Some of the more unusual combinations are the Green Tea Wonut, which includes matcha powder and is topped with candied ginger and pistachio nuts, and the Chocolate Turtle Wonut, which crowns a chocolate cake with thick caramel and chopped pecans. In addition, there are vegan and gluten-free Wonuts.

But the creativity at Waffles Café doesn't end with the Wonut. Some of the popular breakfast dishes include sharp-Cheddar-flavored waffles topped with braised short ribs and scallions and meatballs served on a queso fresco waffle with spicy tomato sauce. The lunch menu includes vegetarian options like a quinoa burger and a black bean burger, along with the beef and bison, and the panini grouping on the menu includes a BLT made with the same peppered bacon that tops the Maple Wonut.

If Charles Caleb Colton was correct that "imitation is truly the sincerest form of flattery," Hernandez and his Wonut should be very flattered indeed. Within weeks of news of his invention appearing online, shops from Maine to Maui were starting to copy the format.

There are two Waffles Café locations.

DO-RITE DONUTS & COFFEE

Do-Rite Donuts wants customers to receive yeast-raised, cake, and old-fashioned treats while they're still warm. They're cooked in batches of thirty-six because the small fryers only hold twenty at a time. It's no surprise that this insistence on quality carries over from the freshness of the donuts to the ingredients hand-selected to go into them.

But what does surprise donut devotees is that Do-Rite is bankrolled by Lettuce Entertain You Enterprises (LEYE), a company that has been opening restaurants known for theatrical flair and good food value since 1971. Small concepts, like donut shops that close when they've run out of dough for the day, are not the LEYE model.

Do-Rite is the brainchild of Jeff Mahin and Francis Brennan, who opened the first shop in 2012, and while they maintain that they're "not reinventing the wheel, we're just making donuts," many of the customers beg to differ.

The Boston Cream Pie totally breaks from the traditional mold. The donut itself is a chocolate almond bar that is filled with almond pastry cream before being dipped into chocolate and sprinkled with toasted almonds. While maple bacon is now commonplace on donut menus, at Do-Rite the base donut is a light and airy French cruller that is given a bath in maple glaze before bits of candied bacon are added.

Old-fashioned donuts are hardly stepchildren at this shop. The basic buttermilk old-fashioned is glazed with either chocolate or lemon, but don't

Do-Rite Donuts & Coffee
50 West Randolph Street
Chicago, Illinois 60601
(312) 488-2483

Do-Rite Donuts & Chicken
233 East Erie Street
Chicago, Illinois 60654
(312) 344-1374

www.doritedonuts.com

miss the chocolate dough variation, which is dipped into molten Valrhona chocolate after it emerges from the fryer.

Offerings built on yeast-raised dough include one with a vanilla bean glaze, a bar filled with coconut cream and topped with toasted coconut, and a glazed donut scented with cinnamon and rolled in cinnamon streusel.

Cake donuts are also glorified here. There's a carrot cake donut topped with cream cheese frosting and a crunchy pistachio-coated cake donut that includes tangy Meyer lemon and chopped pistachios in the dough. Many of the donuts also are made in gluten-free and vegan versions.

The same donuts are available at the second shop, which opened in the summer of 2014, but the menu there also features fried chicken sandwiches. The chicken cutlets are brined before being fried and the spicy version is topped with jalapeño aïoli sauce.

ENDGRAIN

Enoch Simpson began frying up donuts to feed the line cooks when he was sous chef at Nightwood. They ended up on the menu, and Enoch became known as "the guy who does those incredible butterscotch bacon donuts."

He and his brother, Caleb, a master woodworker, were planning to open a donut shop following his stint working for Stephanie Izard at Girl & the Goat, when the space for a fifty-seat restaurant in the Roscoe Village neighborhood became available. Thus was born Endgrain, which takes on different personalities depending on the time of day. In the morning, it's a coffee and donut shop staffed by baristas and not servers; the Bloody Marys flow when it's time for weekend brunch; and the menu becomes that of a full-scale New American restaurant in the evenings, after the oil used to fry the donuts is replaced by oil to fry chicken.

The two brothers built the restaurant, which opened in June 2013, themselves. The name comes from the pieces of endgrain reclaimed lumber used to build the bar, which is fashioned so that one end becomes a peninsula forming a table for six. The same lumberyard woodbin look, with exposed wooden block ends, dominates one wall, and over it hangs a stuffed boar head. The light fixtures are vintage poultry feeders, and the austere space is warmed by all the visible wooden textures.

The two donuts that are signatures for Endgrain are the butterscotch-bacon Enoch devised

Endgrain
1851 West Addison Street
Chicago, Illinois 60613
(773) 687-8191

www.endgrainrestaurant.com

almost a decade ago and the bourbon vanilla. "Those two are always made first thing," says Enoch. But that's hardly the end of his repertoire. In the cake donut camp are such flavors as glazed pumpkin with spiced pepitas, carrot cake donut, and Nutella chocolate cake donut made with stout beer.

Enoch's yeast donuts include salted caramel, German chocolate with toasted coconut, chocolate turtle with caramel frosting and walnut praline, and bear claws stuffed with homemade jams.

The donuts go on sale at 7:00 a.m., and the weekend brunch menu starts at 9:00 a.m. But late brunchers cannot be assured that the donuts will be available—once they've sold out, the case is not restocked—so while diners may linger, they usually begin ordering before noon.

Enoch is as famous for his biscuits as his donuts, and he watched thousands of YouTube videos of old Southern grandmothers making biscuits to refine his technique. Biscuits and gravy—enlivened with some Moroccan harissa— are the backbone of brunch, and biscuit sandwiches made with everything from smoked trout to pork belly to fried chicken are also good options. Enoch makes miniature biscuits and threads them onto skewers with cubes of cheddar and ham as a garnish for Bloody Marys, too.

It was only natural, with his dual interest in donuts and biscuits, that a hybrid would emerge, and the doughscuit, born a few months after the restaurant opened, is the love child of the two. The dough is a variation on biscuit dough, but the circles are fried. They are cut in half through the middle—like a biscuit—and filled with crème fraîche and either chocolate ganache or pastry cream before being glazed.

Very soon after its birth, the doughscuit won top honors at Donut Fest, where it was judged by a panel of restaurateurs and a Chicago police officer.

GLAM DOLL DONUTS

MINNEAPOLIS, MINNESOTA

The area surrounding the Minneapolis Institute of Arts—dubbed "Eat Street"—is home to dozens of small independent restaurants. That's where you'll find Glam Doll Donuts, the captivating shop opened in February 2013, owned and run by Teresa Fox and Arwyn Birch.

While many donut shops have an asterisk following their posted hours that means "or until sold out," Glam Doll Donuts caters to the young night owls who frequent this part of the city with consistently late hours and an array of whimsically named yeast-raised donuts, crullers, fritters, and cake donuts. The shop opens at 7:00 a.m. daily, and it's open until 1:00 a.m. on weekends. Sunday afternoon is the only day that closing time occurs while it's still light.

Style is the focus of Glam Doll Donuts, from the interior of the light and airy shop—featuring a coral-colored ceiling and black-and-white tile steps—to the intense colors and equally intense fla-

Glam Doll Donuts
2605 Nicollet Avenue
Minneapolis, Minnesota 55408
(612) 345-7064

www.glamdolldonuts.com

vors of the donuts filling the case. There are vintage fashion magazines on the walls, there's a photo booth in the back that still functions, and the uniforms (designed by Arwyn) have the retro look of a 1950s diner.

The whimsical names given the donuts make ordering part of the fun.

The Chart Topper, for example, combines peanut butter and chopped peanuts with squiggles of fiery sriracha sauce, and the Flirty Frenchie is a cruller topped with lines of chocolate and stars made from cream cheese flavored with espresso. Spicy and sweet also meet in the Bombshell, a spicy

Mexican chocolate donut topped with homemade cayenne pecan halves.

"There are a lot of Asian and Mexican cafes and markets in the neighborhood, and we draw inspiration from their wide range of ingredients," says Teresa.

Bacon is now as important a garnish for donuts as glazes and sprinkles. At Glam Doll Donuts, it's used in a few ways. The Pinup Girl is a bourbon apple fritter topped with glaze and bacon, while the Scream Queen uses bacon as the topping on a cake donut crowned with chocolate ganache.

Glam Doll also offers a number of vegan donuts made with coconut milk and cornstarch. One of the most popular choices in that line is the Misfit, a yeast-raised donut lavished with a glaze infused with cinnamon, ginger, and orange.

Everything is made from scratch every day in the kitchen, and all of the dairy products are from a local dairy that has been in operation for decades. This attention to quality was recognized a mere few months after the shop opened, when *City Pages* selected Glam Doll's offerings as the best donuts in the city of Minneapolis.

Teresa and Arwyn have been best friends for more than two decades, and since Teresa's grandmother always provided cake donuts for the munching, Arwyn was always there to enjoy them. As an adult, Arwyn became involved with vintage clothing and design, and it's her vision that shaped the distinctive look of Glam Doll Donuts.

Glam Doll Donuts is about fantasy and fun. But the donuts are seriously delicious.

LINDSTROM BAKERY

Minnesota was the epicenter of immigration from the Scandinavian countries during the nineteenth century, and it's still where you'll find the best concentration of baked goods drawn from that rich culinary heritage. One of those forms is donuts, and they are the most famous offering from Lindstrom Bakery.

The bakery has been here for more than forty years, and the founder, Donald Coulombe, developed the recipe for the donuts. His wife, Bernetta, whom everyone calls Bernie, still runs the business, and now son Mark is involved, too.

"Both his mom and dad were bakers, his uncle was a baker, and he was a baker in the army," says Bernie. It was the Scandinavian donuts that she says "really launched and built our business." They come plain, glazed, dusted with cinnamon sugar, and iced with chocolate.

While donuts may be the claim to fame, the bakery also makes traditional breads—limpa scented with orange, raisin rye, hot cross buns around Easter—and cookies. And while in other parts of the country fruitcakes may have turned into a holiday joke, they remain a popular option here and are advertised as made with "butter, rum, brandy, pineapples, cherries, and pecans. No dates, raisins, or citron."

Lindstrom Bakery
12830 Lake Boulevard
Lindström, Minnesota 55045
(651) 257-1374

The village of Lindström, located 35 miles northeast of Minneapolis, was first settled by Daniel Lindström in 1853 and was incorporated forty years later. The village of 4,500 adopted the motto "America's Little Sweden," and most of the families are of Scandinavian, if not Swedish, heritage.

SCANDINAVIAN DONUTS

Makes 12 to 15

6 large eggs, at room temperature

2 cups granulated sugar, divided

3 tablespoons unsalted butter, melted and cooled

⅓ cup heavy whipping cream

1 tablespoon brandy

1 teaspoon baking soda

1 teaspoon ground cardamom, divided

¼ teaspoon baking powder

Pinch of salt

6 cups all-purpose flour, plus more for dusting

Vegetable oil for frying

WHILE DONALD COULOMBE'S recipe at Lindstrom Bakery is a closely guarded secret, the various descriptions of the donut place it in the tradition of two beloved Norwegian donuts, *smul-tringer* and *hjortebakkels*. Both are cake donuts made with many more eggs than traditional American cake or old-fashioned donuts. Like many Scandinavian baked goods, they contain aromatic ground cardamom.

Beat the eggs in a stand mixer with the whisk attachment until thick and light yellow in color. Switch to the paddle attachment, and beat in 1⅓ cups of the sugar. Beat at medium speed for 2 minutes. Add the butter, cream, brandy, baking soda, ½ teaspoon of the cardamom, baking powder, and salt. Beat until well combined.

Add the flour and beat at low speed until thoroughly combined. Grease a large sheet of plastic wrap and scrape the dough into the center. Make the dough into a round pancake about 1 inch thick. Refrigerate the dough for at least 1 hour, or up to 24 hours.

Dust a surface and rolling pin with flour. Roll the chilled dough to a thickness of ½ inch. Use a donut cutter dipped in flour to cut out as many donuts as possible; alternatively, use a 2½-inch cookie cutter and then cut out holes with a ½-inch cutter. Transfer the donuts and holes carefully to a baking sheet sprinkled with flour. Reroll the scraps one time to a thickness of ½ inch and cut out more donuts and holes. Allow the donuts to sit for 10 minutes to dry the exteriors slightly.

Heat at least 2 inches of oil to a temperature of 350°F in a Dutch oven or deep skillet. Place a few layers of paper towels on a baking sheet and top it with a wire cooling rack.

(recipe continues)

Carefully slide a few donuts into the hot oil, being careful not to crowd the pan and making sure that the donuts do not touch each other. Fry the donuts for 2 minutes per side, or until evenly browned.

Drain the donuts on the rack, blotting them gently with additional paper towels. Fry the remaining donuts and the donut holes in the same manner.

Mix the remaining sugar and remaining cardamom in a shallow bowl. Once the donuts are cool enough to handle, coat them in the bowl of cardamom sugar. Serve as soon as possible.

The donut dough can be refrigerated for up to 2 days. Do not form or fry the donuts until just prior to serving.

Cardamom is found in cuisines as diverse as those of India, North Africa, and Scandinavia. It's an aromatic and assertive spice made by grinding the seeds found encased in its pods. While the flavor of cardamom is distinctive, it can be replicated by substituting a mixture of equal parts ground cinnamon, ground allspice, and freshly grated nutmeg.

THE DONUT WHOLE

You can get a round-the-clock donut fix at this shop in the Douglas Design District of downtown Wichita. While the shop closes from midnight to 6:00 a.m., the drive-thru still operates because cooks are there preparing donuts for the next day.

But this shop, which opened in 2009, is more of a neighborhood hangout than purely a place that dispenses donuts. Local artists hang their works on the walls and local musicians play concerts on Friday and Saturday nights. The Donut Whole is all about fun—and delicious donuts.

The fun is advertised the moment customers walk in the door and see the space, which can only be described as high kitsch. There's signage and a fiberglass lion sculpture rescued from a now-closed amusement park. And it's easy to spot the shop because of its "mascot" mounted on the roof of the building: the giant rooster D.W. "Big Ed" Buttermilk.

Michael Carmody, who grew up near the Oklahoma border, and his partner Angela Mallory, a Wichita native, joined forces and opened the shop in 2009. Michael had previously been selling donuts from his kitchen, and Angela was looking for a new business challenge.

All of their treats start with his recipes for either vanilla or chocolate cake donuts, and the batter relies on local ingredients including butter, buttermilk, and flour milled in nearby Stafford County. In addition, the shop makes vegan donuts every Wednesday, and has since the day it opened.

The owners are constantly experimenting with new flavor combinations and offbeat nuances. The Bumblebee—a chocolate donut topped with a citrus glaze and chocolate sprinkles—gets its name from its gold and brown color combination. The King Midas tops a vanilla donut with Lyle's Golden Syrup (a British import) and crushed salted peanuts, and the Pineapple Upside-Down donut with caramelized fruit remains popular, as does the Donut Whole's version of the ubiquitous maple bacon. The Fluffernutter combines peanut butter and marshmallow as the topping, and peanut butter is joined by grape jam on the PBG.

Every Friday the shop partners with River City Brewery, a microbrewery a few blocks away, to make specialty donuts with their small-batch brews. One week a stout beer with added lactose was used to make a coffee-flavored donut; another

The Donut Whole
1720 East Douglas Avenue
Wichita, Kansas 67214
(316) 262-3700

www.thedonutwhole.com

week a beer infused with berries was amplified in a raspberry donut.

The Donut Whole's owners wanted to create a hip environment where customers will stay a while. There's free Wi-Fi, and customers are encouraged to bring their children during the day and then return on weekend evenings for the free music. The shop's owners are both avid fans of the British science fiction series *Doctor Who,* and they contribute to the cost of showing the series on Wichita's PBS station. They invent donuts to go with the show's plot twists, and they also created an iconic donut for the last episodes of *Breaking Bad.* The vanilla icing was topped with petals of bright blue sugar icing to look like crystal meth.

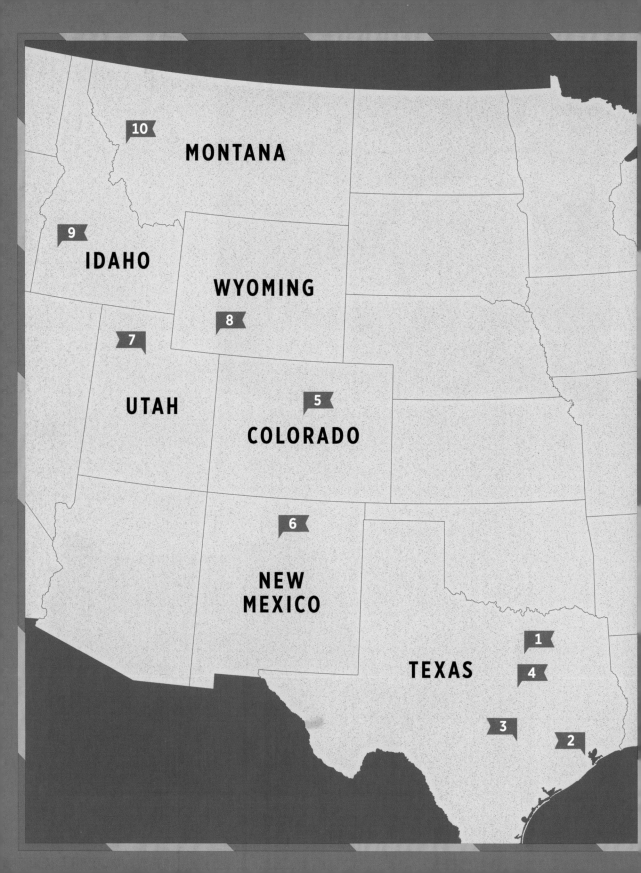

Chapter 5

THE WESTERN STATES

The donuts in the western states, especially in Texas, are truly a mirror of how the American melting pot is reflected in our foods. All of these states have a culinary debt to both the Native Americans and the Spanish who ruled their lands before they became part of the United States.

The Native Americans all had some form of fry bread as an important part of their diets, and these were adopted and transformed by the Spanish and Anglo settlers. The tortilla is the obvious link to that fried legacy, but the sopaipillas of New Mexico are a distinctive donut relative as well.

And then there's the oddity of the "Czech Belt" in Texas, an ethnic community and identity as strong as that of the Pennsylvania Dutch around Philadelphia and the Scandinavians of the Midwest. They are responsible for introducing the kolache throughout the region.

1. HYPNOTIC DONUTS & BISCUITS
2. PEÑA'S DONUT HEAVEN & GRILL
3. GOURDOUGH'S DONUTS
4. CZECH STOP AND LITTLE CZECH BAKERY
5. GLAZED & CONFUZED DONUTS
6. RANCHO DE CHIMAYÓ RESTAURANTÉ
7. BEYOND GLAZE
8. COWBOY DONUTS
9. GURU DONUTS
10. TREASURE STATE DONUTS

HYPNOTIC DONUTS & BISCUITS

Owners James and Amy St. Peter say that the mission of Hypnotic Donuts is to "create the ultimate donut experience and have fun along the way." How could one not have fun while eating Jenny's Evil Elvis, a yeast-raised donut crowned with a combination of peanut butter, banana, bacon, and honey? Or if that's not your passion, there's the Triple 6, a vanilla cake donut topped with passion fruit–habañero icing, and the Expresso Yo-Self, a chocolate cake donut topped with coffee icing and drizzles of salted caramel and sprinkled with freshly ground coffee.

A shop favorite is the Peace'statio, which is a cake donut with a brown butter glaze and chopped pistachio nuts. Customers also clamor for the Maui Waui, a long john stuffed with coconut cream and topped with a vanilla bean glaze and toasted coconut.

In addition, Hypnotic Donuts creates a whole line of vegan donuts and cinnamon buns on Mondays and Tuesdays. James says that there were requests for vegan pastries before the shop even opened, and while there were a number of bakeries in Austin offering vegan treats, they were the first in Dallas to make them on a regular basis.

The St. Peters began selling donuts out of the back of their SUV in 2010. They then shared a storefront with a pizza shop before opening their Dallas shop in January 2012. In addition to a wide array of yeast-raised and cake donuts, the menu includes fritters loaded with fresh fruits and long johns

stuffed with many flavors of house-made creamy fillings. A second location in Denton, about forty miles north of Dallas, opened in the fall of 2014.

James and Amy think of their customers as family, and they refer to them as the Hyppies. While the Dallas shop closes in the early afternoon, on Wednesday nights they reopen for "BYOB Bingo," at which donuts are served (of course!) and participants are encouraged to bring the beverages of their choice.

The second part of the shop's name comes from the line of biscuits that Amy bakes each day while James works on the donuts. For something savory to go with the donuts, there is an entire line of chicken biscuits. The chicken breast is marinated for a day before being cooked fresh for each order, and the flavor combinations are as imaginative as those for the donuts.

The Amy has chicken layered with bacon, pickles, spicy mustard, Cheddar, and honey, while the Kaye's chicken fillet is topped with whipped cream cheese, fresh jalapeño peppers, and pepper Jack cheese.

If you're not looking for chicken, however, you can still enjoy a biscuit. The Down Home features peppery white gravy made in house, and the Grab and Go is biscuit dough wrapped around homemade sage sausage and then baked. It's Hypnotic Donuts' version of a sausage roll.

Perhaps the most iconic dish at Hypnotic Donuts & Biscuits is the chicken sandwich called the Jim. In lieu of a biscuit, it's served on a glazed donut that has been split, toasted, and then turned upside down so that the honey glaze melts into the hot fried chicken.

Hypnotic Donuts has two locations.

9007 Garland Road
Dallas, Texas 75218
(214) 668-6999

235 West Hickory Street
Denton, Texas 76201
(817) 403-0356

CHOCOLATE CAKE DONUTS
WITH COFFEE GLAZE

Makes 12

DONUTS

3 cups all-purpose flour, divided, plus more for dusting

¾ cup unsweetened cocoa powder

¾ cup granulated sugar

¼ cup firmly packed light brown sugar

2 teaspoons baking powder

1 teaspoon baking soda

½ teaspoon salt

1 large egg, at room temperature

2 large egg yolks, at room temperature

¾ cup buttermilk

¾ teaspoon pure vanilla extract

6 tablespoons unsalted butter, melted and cooled

Vegetable oil for frying

GLAZE AND TOPPING

2 tablespoons instant espresso powder (or substitute instant coffee granules)

1¾ cups confectioners' sugar

1 tablespoon light corn syrup

¼ teaspoon pure vanilla extract

Pinch of salt

2 tablespoons finely ground espresso coffee beans

EVERY COOK SHOULD have an intensely flavored chocolate cake donut in his or her repertoire, and this one is my favorite. It could form the base for Hypnotic Donuts' favorite, the Expresso Yo-Self, with the included coffee glaze and a sprinkling of finely ground coffee.

Combine 1 cup of the flour with the cocoa powder, granulated sugar, light brown sugar, baking powder, baking soda, and salt in the bowl of a stand mixer fitted with the paddle attachment, and mix well at low speed. Combine the egg, egg yolks, buttermilk, vanilla, and melted butter in a small bowl and whisk well.

Add the wet ingredients to the dry ingredients and beat at medium speed to mix well. Add the remaining flour and beat at low speed until the flour is blended in and no white streaks remain. Scrape the dough onto a sheet of floured plastic wrap and pat it into a circle that is 1 inch thick. Refrigerate the dough for at least 2 hours, or up to 24 hours.

While the dough chills, prepare the glaze. Pour the espresso powder into ¼ cup of very hot tap water, and stir to dissolve it. Combine the mixture with the confectioners' sugar, corn syrup, vanilla, and salt in a mixing bowl and whisk until smooth. Press a sheet of plastic wrap directly into the surface to keep the glaze from hardening.

Heat at least 2 inches of oil to a temperature of 350°F in a Dutch oven or deep skillet. Place a few layers of paper towels on a baking sheet and top it with a wire cooling rack.

While the oil heats, dust a surface and rolling pin generously with flour. Roll the chilled dough to a thickness of ½ inch. Use a donut cutter dipped in flour to cut out as many donuts as possible; alternatively, use a 2½-inch cookie cutter and then cut out holes with a

(recipe continues)

$\frac{1}{2}$-inch cutter. Transfer the donuts and holes carefully to a baking sheet sprinkled with flour. Reroll the scraps one time to a thickness of $\frac{1}{2}$ inch and cut out more donuts and holes.

Carefully slide a few donuts into the hot oil, being careful not to crowd the pan and making sure that the donuts do not touch each other. Once the donuts float to the top of the oil, fry them for 1 to $1\frac{1}{2}$ minutes per side, or until evenly browned.

Drain the donuts on the rack, blotting them gently with additional paper towels. Fry the remaining donuts and the donut holes in the same manner. While the donuts are still warm, dip the tops into the glaze, turning to coat them well. Place them with the glazed side up on a wire rack set over a sheet of waxed paper. Sprinkle the ground coffee on top of the glaze. Let the donuts stand for 20 minutes, or until the glaze is set.

The cut-out donuts can be refrigerated for up to 1 day, lightly covered with plastic wrap. They should not be fried or glazed more than 6 hours prior to serving.

PEÑA'S DONUT HEAVEN & GRILL

Pearland is part of Houston's metropolitan sprawl, yet the town of about 100,000 retains the feel of a small community. The middle school is named for Texas Rangers pitcher Nolan Ryan, and many of the residents work nearby at the Texas Medical Center or at NASA's Johnson Space Center. And an integral part of their identity as residents of Pearland is bringing the family to Peña's Donut Heaven & Grill a few times a week for breakfast or lunch, and, of course, donuts.

Ray Peña's mother, Josie, owned a donut shop where he started working at the age of nineteen. He and his wife, Debbie, knew that a donut shop was in their future, but for twenty years Ray was a firefighter who thought about donuts more than he made them.

Peña's Donut Heaven & Grill
11601 Shadow Creek Parkway
Pearland, Texas 77584
(713) 340-3231

www.donutheavenandgrill.com

Ray opened his first Donut Heaven shop in 1996, and he moved to his present location in 2010. There are now more than thirty types of donuts produced each day, plus both savory and sweet kolaches and his hybrid donut and croissant, called a "dosant."

"Every dough, every glaze, and every filling are made in-house," says Ray. And the range is almost mind-boggling. In addition to custard and jelly donut fillings ranging from coconut to strawberry to lemon, there are bear claws and baked cinnamon rolls, too. Some of the glazed donuts are topped with morsels of sweet breakfast cereal like Cocoa Puffs and Fruit Loops.

The dosants have a cream cheese filling, and they are usually topped with confectioners' sugar and fresh fruits, including all sorts of berries and even banana.

While kolaches are a Czech pastry, they are a fixture in donut shops all over Texas. Ray's kolaches are savory, which makes them technically *klobasniky*. But while that distinction may be honored in the Czech Republic, in Texas they're all kolaches, whether the filling is cherry or chorizo. The kolaches at Peña's were selected by *Houston* magazine as one of the hundred top dishes in the region. The not-traditionally-Czech fillings on offer include sausage, cheese, and jalapeño; chorizo, egg, and cheese; and a Cajun option filled with boudin sausage.

What differentiates Peña's Donut Heaven & Grill from other donut shops is the extensive grill side of the menu. For breakfast, there are many variations on the Texas classic, breakfast tacos, and included among the breakfast sandwiches is one with sausage, egg, and cheese served on a glazed donut.

Peña's is also famous for its burgers, for which the buns are baked fresh each morning. Some of the combinations include Ray's Frito Pie Burger, which includes chili, cheese, grilled onions, jalapeños, and mustard as toppings, and the Olé Burger, made with chipotle mayonnaise, queso fresco, pico de gallo, and jalapeños. There are also bison, turkey, and vegetarian burgers. Cheeseburgers can also be served on a glazed donut.

The latest addition to the menu is Funnel Fries. Made with a funnel cake batter, they're fried in strips, resulting in something like a French fry sprinkled with confectioners' sugar instead of salt, and served with a cup of sweet sauce for dipping.

GOURDOUGH'S DONUTS

★ **AUSTIN, TEXAS** ★

"Big. Fat. Donuts." There are times that the motto says it all, and that's the case with this donut shop housed in a vintage silver 1978 Airstream trailer. Not only are the donuts big and fat, they're also some of the most creative in the country, and they're fried to order.

They may not win any beauty contests. The toppings are loaded on rather than artfully arranged. But the flavor combinations and sheer size of the donuts emerging from the window at Gourdough's are what tantalizes.

Gourdough's, which opened in the fall of 2009, is the brainchild of Ryan Palmer and Paula Samford. They began making donuts with outrageous toppings at home, and soon friends started calling to request a batch. They perfected the yeast-raised recipe, and then they turned their creative talents to the toppings and fanciful names.

There's the Funky Monkey, which is topped with cream cheese icing and grilled bananas given a brûlée treatment with some brown sugar. And then there's the Carney, which marries apple pie topping, roasted peanuts, and caramel to form the topping.

Fruit plays a role in many of the combinations, too. Miss Shortcake is topped with cream cheese icing and a veritable mound of sliced fresh strawberries. Customers can enjoy strawberries grilled on top of a thick layer of fudge icing in the Dirty Berry.

Gourdough's
1503 South 1st Street
Austin, Texas 78704
(512) 707-1050

www.gourdoughs.com

Gourdough's Public House
2700 South Lamar Boulevard
Austin, Texas 78704
(512) 912-9070

www.gourdoughspub.com

Gourdough's is known for its combinations of savory and sweet toppings. The Mother Clucker is related to the popular Southern dish fried chicken and waffles. In this case, morsels of fried chicken are arranged on a donut, and then the whole thing is drizzled heavily with honey butter. The Flying Pig is Gordough's version of the ubiquitous maple bacon donut, but it is not the only porcine option. Porkey's layers jalapeño jelly and cream cheese on top of the donut and then finishes it with crispy slices of Canadian bacon.

And while the existing combinations are unique enough for most palates, customers also have the option of designing a fantasy donut with their choice of a filling, an icing, and up to three toppings.

Gourdough's is open from early morning until late at night, and two years after lighting the flames under the fryers, Paula and Ryan cashed in their donut fame to start an actual brick-and-mortar restaurant. The menu at Gourdough's Public House includes some of the combinations that brought the trailer its fame, but it is expanded to include many options that require a real kitchen to produce.

All of the Public House's sandwiches, burgers, and entrées are served on top of a hot donut. The choices include the Dirty South, a chicken-fried steak with cream gravy and cranberry habañero jam, and the Nacho Libre Burger, topped with spicy refried beans, chili, cheese sauce, and Fritos.

But diners should always save room for dessert. While the trailer's ode to chocolate is named the Black Out, diners in the restaurant can finish a meal with the Ring O' Fire. The chocolate is infused with chipotle chiles, and then cayenne candied pecans are sprinkled liberally over the salted caramel sauce.

CZECH STOP AND LITTLE CZECH BAKERY

WEST, TEXAS

A corridor along what is now I-35 in south-central Texas, between Dallas and Austin, has been dubbed the "Czech Belt" because of large waves of mid-nineteenth-century immigration from Central Europe to the region. The little village of West, about twenty miles north of Waco, still maintains a sense of this Tex-Czech culture, with about 70 percent of the residents tracing their lineage to the Czech Republic. And for more than thirty years, West has been home to the Czech Stop and its adjoining Little Czech Bakery, where kolaches are made the same way they were more than a century ago.

The kolache (pronounced *koh-LAH-chee*) was traditionally popular in Midwestern states with Czech populations, and they are now enjoying expanded visibility nationally (Brooklyn Kolache Company, page 73, and Cowboy Donuts, page 193).

Czech Stop and
Little Czech Bakery
105 North College Avenue
West, Texas 76691
(254) 826-4161

www.czechstop.net

But these baked sweet or savory yeast-raised pastries are most popular in Texas, where they are viewed as the quintessential road food.

Kolaches are served 24/7 at Czech Stop, which also sells gas and the sundries of all roadside convenience stores. "When Bill Polk started it back in 1983, it was a combination gas station, snack bar, and liquor store," recalls current owner Barbara Schissler, who was Polk's only employee for many years. "Groups like MADD (Mothers Against

Drunk Driving) really came down hard because we're so close to the Interstate, so Bill closed the liquor store portion in 1985 and turned it into the bakery," she says, adding that they still sell beer and wine.

Even though the same menu is available from both sides of the building, there is frequently a line. Czech Stop is not automated fast food, and locals are willing to wait even if transients complain. That's because locals know how delicious the treats are.

On the sweet side of the case are fruit kolaches, as well as those filled with poppy seeds and sweetened cream cheese. These are the traditional forms that the Czech people brought to Texas.

But kolache now also include pastries with savory fillings: cheese, kielbasa, and jalapeño peppers, for example, or eggs and sausage. While kolache were brought here by Czech immigrants, it was their Texan descendants who thought to wrap pastry around a sausage. In addition to the quasi-authentic combinations, Czech Stop offers savory kolache filled with barbecued pulled pork and a pizza-like combination of pepperoni, mozzarella, and tomato sauce.

Another category of sandwiches, called the Hot Chubbies, are stuffed with savories like roast beef, salami, or cheese that are baked in the bun. The bakery also collects rave reviews for the full line of quick breads, especially the zucchini bread and cherry pecan bread, as well as for its strudels and cookies.

Eating at Czech Stop is also an educational experience. All of the flavors of kolaches are listed in Czech as well as English. So if you ever wondered what the Czech word was for "apple," you leave knowing it's *jablkové*. But you're in luck ordering a loaf of pumpernickel bread: the word is the same in both languages.

KOLACHES KEEP A COMMUNITY GOING

If the name West, Texas, rings a bell, it's probably not because of kolaches. West was the site of the explosion at the West Fertilizer Company plant at 8:00 p.m. on April 17, 2013. Emergency personnel were responding to a call that there was a fire at the plant when the explosion occurred, killing fifteen people and seriously injuring more than 160.

Barbara Schissler had the power to the Czech Stop gas pumps cut because she feared another explosion. Then she started tending to the wounded and first responders who came in throughout the night and into the next day. The shop donated cases of water and handed out free food and drink, as well as donating food to the Red Cross.

A tragedy like the explosion rocks a small community. Some employees lost their homes, and many personally knew those who were killed or injured. But Barbara made sure the kolaches and coffee kept coming for all who wandered in seeking refuge.

KOLACHES

Makes 16

DOUGH

1 (¼-ounce) package active dry yeast

1 cup whole milk, heated to 110°F to 115°F, divided

⅓ cup granulated sugar

3½ cups all-purpose flour, divided, plus more for dusting

10 tablespoons (1¼ sticks) unsalted butter, melted, divided

1 large egg

2 large egg yolks

½ teaspoon salt

FILLING

¾ cup (6 ounces) cream cheese, at room temperature

1 large egg yolk

3 tablespoons granulated sugar

2 tablespoons all-purpose flour

½ teaspoon grated lemon zest

½ teaspoon pure vanilla extract

TOPPING

2 tablespoons all-purpose flour

2 tablespoons firmly packed light brown sugar

1 tablespoon unsalted butter, at room temperature

Pinch of salt

AUTHENTIC CZECH KOLACHES are wonderful homey pastries. The dough is rich with butter and eggs, but not overly sweet. What I've given you here is the traditional cream cheese filling, but you can use any sort of fruit jam instead of or in conjunction with the cheese.

For the dough, combine the yeast, ½ cup warm milk, sugar, and ½ cup flour in the bowl of a stand mixer fitted with the paddle attachment, and mix well. Set aside for about 10 minutes while the yeast proofs.

When the yeast looks frothy, add the remaining milk, remaining flour, 8 tablespoons of the butter, egg, egg yolks, and salt, and beat at low speed until the flour is incorporated, forming a soft dough.

Place the dough hook on the mixer, and knead the dough at medium speed for 2 minutes. Raise the speed to medium-high, and knead for an additional 3 to 4 minutes, or until the dough forms a soft ball and is springy. (If kneading by hand, this will take about 12 to 15 minutes.)

Lightly grease the inside of a large mixing bowl with softened butter or vegetable oil. Add the dough, turning it so it is lightly greased all over. Cover the bowl loosely with a sheet of oiled plastic wrap or a damp tea towel, and place it in a warm, draft-free spot. Allow the dough to rise for 1 to 2 hours, or until it has doubled in bulk.

While the dough rises, make the filling and topping. For the filling, combine the cream cheese, egg yolk, sugar, flour, lemon zest, and vanilla in a mixing bowl and beat at medium speed with an electric mixer to combine. Increase the speed to high, and beat until light and fluffy. Set aside. For the topping, combine the flour, sugar, butter, and salt in a small bowl. Work the mixture with your fingers until it resembles breadcrumbs. Set aside.

(recipe continues)

Line two baking sheets with parchment paper or silicone baking mats. Punch the dough down and divide it into 16 equal parts. Grease your hands and roll each part into a tight ball. Arrange 8 balls on each baking sheet, tapping down the top of each slightly. Cover the baking sheets with sheets of oiled plastic wrap and allow the kolaches to rise for 30 to 40 minutes, or until they are almost doubled in bulk.

Preheat the oven to 375°F. Make an indentation in the top of each kolache with the back of a soup spoon and fill it with a heaping tablespoonful of the cheese filling. Lightly brush the exterior with the remaining melted butter and then sprinkle with the topping.

Bake the kolaches for 15 to 17 minutes, or until golden brown, switching the position of the baking sheets midway through the time. Allow the kolaches to cool on the baking sheet for 10 minutes. Then serve immediately.

The kolaches can be baked up to 6 hours in advance and kept at room temperature, lightly covered with plastic wrap.

GLAZED & CONFUZED DONUTS

In two years the "donut artists" at Glazed & Confuzed Donuts went from selling at a few farmers' markets to their own shop, plus a business supplying coffee shops around the city. And what has led to their pinnacle of popularity in the Mile High City are such donuts as the Mojito, glazed with a combination of rum, lime zest, and mint and decorated with a candied mint leaf; the Confuzed Car Bomb, filled with custard laced with Bailey's Irish Cream and coated with a Guinness glaze and mint chocolate chips; and Root Beer Float. The Float is filled with vanilla cream, and the glaze contains root beer extract from a local bottler. It's topped with some molecular gastronomy magic that looks like soda foam but holds its shape and texture for hours.

Glazed & Confuzed is truly a family project. Josh Schwab, a Los Angeles native and a graduate of Le Cordon Bleu in Pasadena, California, worked as a baker in Hawaii at Roy Yamaguchi's Roy's Hawaiian Fusion for two years. While there he met Ben Hafdahl, who grew up in Duluth, Minnesota, on the shores of Lake Superior. Ben had more front-of-the-house experience and was working as food and beverage director at a hotel in Las Vegas when Josh called to lure him into the donut business. They were certainly familiar with each other as people, not only from their time at Roy's, but because Josh's wife, Farah, and Ben's wife, Sarah, are sisters. While Farah kept her job as an ultrasound technician, Sarah, who

Glazed & Confuzed Donuts
5301 Leetdale Drive
Denver, Colorado
(303) 524-9637

www.gcdonuts.com

was formerly a glass blower at the Corning Museum in New York, is the third partner making donuts daily.

Some of Glazed & Confuzed's most popular choices are cake donuts. The Breaking Banana Bread, topped with a creamy caramel glaze sprinkled with sea salt, can also be enjoyed another way as the Bananas Foster, topped with rum-spiked brown sugar glaze and slices of bananas flambéed on the top. Another popular cake donut is Da Killa' Carrot Cake: The spiced donut made with fresh carrots has ginger cream in its center and is topped with a vanilla glaze and house-made toffee walnuts.

Josh's own version of the trending donut-croissant hybrid is called the PuffyNutz. Order one served as the Tiramisu, which is stuffed with sweet mascarpone filling and spread with a creamy espresso glaze topped with a sprinkling of espresso powder.

In today's world of donuts, an option incorporating bacon is as de rigueur as a plain glazed, and Glazed & Confused has one called Breakfast of Champz. What they claim differentiates it from the competition is that the bacon flavor is infused into the glaze as well as forming crunchy nuggets on top of it.

The three bakers produce eight flavors of donuts a day, plus a PuffyNutz, vegan donuts, and gluten-free donuts. Josh is fond of saying that "these aren't your Daddy's donuts," and few could argue while eating an Olé!, a yeast-raised donut topped with chipotle chocolate ganache and crushed tortilla chips in three colors.

CARROT CAKE DONUTS

Makes 16

¾ cup whole milk

1 cup finely chopped carrot

1 cup chopped walnuts
or pecans

3½ cups all-purpose flour,
plus more for dusting

4 teaspoons baking powder

1 teaspoon ground cinnamon

¾ teaspoon salt

⅔ cup granulated sugar

2 large eggs, at room
temperature

4 tablespoons (½ stick)
unsalted butter, melted and
cooled

1 teaspoon pure vanilla extract

½ cup chopped raisins

Vegetable oil for frying

Cream Cheese Icing
(page 117)

GLAZED & CONFUZED DONUTS touts the donut form of carrot cake—complete with cream cheese icing—as one of its specialties. When I was working on this recipe, I discovered that simmering the carrot in the milk accomplished two purposes: It cooked the carrot, because the time it takes for a donut to fry is far shorter than for a carrot to cook, and it also infused the milk with the carrot's sweet flavor.

Combine the milk and carrot in a small saucepan and bring to a simmer over medium heat, stirring frequently. Reduce the heat to low and simmer the carrot for 5 minutes, or until the pieces are tender. Remove the pan from the heat and allow the mixture to cool.

Preheat the oven to 350°F. Toast the nuts on a baking sheet for 5 to 7 minutes, or until fragrant and brown. Remove the pan from the oven and set aside.

Combine the flour, baking powder, cinnamon, salt, and sugar in the bowl of a stand mixer fitted with the paddle attachment. Mix on low to combine the ingredients. Add the cooled carrot mixture, eggs, butter, and vanilla to the mixer and beat at medium speed for 1 minute. Fold in the raisins and ½ cup of the toasted nuts.

Scrape the dough onto a sheet of floured plastic wrap and pat it into a 1-inch-thick circle. Refrigerate the dough for at least 2 hours, or up to 24 hours.

Heat at least 2 inches of oil to a temperature of 360°F in a Dutch oven or deep skillet. Place a few layers of paper towels on a baking sheet and top it with a wire cooling rack.

While the oil heats, dust a surface and rolling pin with flour. Roll the chilled dough to a thickness of ½ inch. Use a donut cutter dipped in flour to cut out as many donuts as possible; alternatively, use a 2½-inch cookie cutter and then cut out holes with a ½-inch cutter.

(recipe continues)

Transfer the donuts and holes carefully to a baking sheet sprinkled with flour. Reroll the scraps one time to a thickness of 1/2 inch and cut out more donuts and holes.

Carefully slide a few donuts into the hot oil, being careful not to crowd the pan and making sure that the donuts do not touch each other. Once the donuts float to the top of the oil, fry them for 1 to 1½ minutes per side, or until evenly browned.

Drain the donuts on the rack, blotting them gently with additional paper towels. Fry the remaining donuts and the donut holes in the same manner.

Allow the donuts to cool completely before frosting them. Sprinkle the frosted donuts with the remaining toasted nuts. Serve immediately.

The dough can be refrigerated for up to 2 days, and the cut-out donuts can also be refrigerated that long, covered with plastic wrap. Do not fry or frost the donuts until just prior to serving.

Rancho de Chimayó is a destination restaurant, but any donut lover will be thankful it was their destination after eating the sopaipillas. These feather-light pillows of fried dough can be eaten plain when they are placed on the table hot in lieu of tortillas or bread, or they can be dipped into local honey for dessert. Sopaipillas are related to many Native American flatbreads, and they're an integral part of the cuisine of this region.

Chimayó, a village of 3,000 located 24 miles north of Santa Fe, is nestled in the Sangre de Cristo mountains. Its name in the Tewa language means "superior red flaking stone," and that stone decomposes to become a rich soil in which the famed Chimayó chiles are grown. The village is also known for textiles woven in traditional Spanish colonial fashion and for the spiritual powers ascribed to its church.

Chimayó has been home to the Jaramillo family since the 1700s, when the distance to Santa Fe and lack of proper roads meant the journey was only undertaken a few times a year. The current *patrón,* Arturo Jaramillo, and his wife, Florence, opened the restaurant in 1965 to serve traditional New Mexican cooking. The restaurant is housed in a century-old adobe building with panoramic

Rancho de Chimayó Restauranté
300 Juan Medina Road
Chimayó, New Mexico 87522
(505) 984-2100

www.ranchodechimayo.com

mountain views from the terrace during the summer and cozy fireplaces as a backdrop for winter meals when the snow is falling.

Florence Jaramillo wants the restaurant guests to feel "as though they had been invited to an old Spanish home where the food and atmosphere are in the grand early tradition." The tamales, enchiladas, green chile stew, and chiles rellenos cannot be beaten.

While modern diners might raise an eyebrow at the suggestion that shrimp was present in colonial New Mexican cuisine, sopaipillas certainly were. In addition to enjoying them alongside the meal, you can also have one stuffed with shredded beef or chicken and topped with refried beans and guacamole. And no meal at Rancho de Chimayó would be complete without the famous Chimayó cocktail of tequila, locally pressed apple cider, crème de cassis, and lemon juice.

SOPAIPILLAS

Makes 4 dozen

2 cups all-purpose flour,
plus more for dusting

½ teaspoon salt

½ teaspoon baking powder

1 teaspoon granulated sugar

1 tablespoon evaporated milk

2 teaspoons vegetable oil,
plus more for frying

Honey for serving (optional)

SPOONING THE VERY hot oil over the top of the wedges as they fry encourages them to puff up like little pillows. This variation on the fried breads of the Native Americans is moist and tender while also being crisp.

Combine the flour, salt, baking powder, and sugar in the bowl of a standard mixer fitted with the paddle attachment. Blend well, and then add the evaporated milk, vegetable oil, and ¼ cup warm tap water. Beat at low speed to combine, then increase the speed to medium-high and beat for 2 minutes.

Allow the dough to rest for 30 minutes at room temperature.

Divide the dough into 12 parts, and roll each one into a circle on a floured surface with a floured rolling pin to a thickness of ¼ inch. Cut each circle into 4 wedges.

Heat 3 inches of oil to a temperature of 400°F in a Dutch oven or deep skillet. Preheat the oven to 150°F and line a baking sheet with a few layers of paper towels.

Add 4 dough wedges to the hot oil, and spoon the oil over them with a soup ladle or large spoon. After 20 seconds they should be puffed. Turn them over and brown the other side for 15 to 20 seconds. Remove the sopaipillas from the oil with a slotted spatula and drain on the paper towels. Keep the sopaipillas warm in the oven while frying additional batches. Serve immediately, passing honey separately, if using.

The dough can be rolled out up to 1 day in advance and refrigerated with sheets of waxed paper between the layers. Do not fry the sopaipillas until just prior to serving.

BEYOND GLAZE

If it's true that we eat first with our eyes, then the feast at the three Beyond Glaze donut shops in Utah is a banquet before a single choice is made.

Imagine an ethereally light yeast-raised donut, and then on top of it the sort of fancy flair and flourishes one would expect to see on a wedding cake—or at least an ornate cupcake. The frosting is piped in intricate latticework patterns or in the sort of swirls associated with medieval illuminated manuscripts, with contrasting colors dancing before your eyes. And the brilliant colors of the frostings are created from a wide range of real fruit. Like the donuts themselves, the frostings are made fresh in the kitchen with no preservatives of any kind.

The owner of Beyond Glaze is Dean Morgan, who used to run a construction business. When the recession struck the local housing market, he decided it was a sign and he should strike out and do something he had always wanted to do—create wonderful donuts. The original business plan called for a food truck frying donuts on the side of the road, but Dean's daughter, pastry chef Alece Schow, said that the sort of elaborate decoration they planned really needed a shop. The three shops now employ more than two dozen bakers and decorators who spend the day frying and embellishing the donuts.

The underlying aesthetic principle at Beyond Glaze is that the donuts are reasons to celebrate something every day. In the same way that a beau-

2121 South McClelland Street
Salt Lake City, Utah 84106
(801) 355-3495

177 West 12300 South
Draper, Utah 84020
(801) 571-2309

325 24th Street
Ogden, Utah 84401
(801) 675-5714

www.beyondglaze.com

tifully decorated wedding cake is symbolic of the experience, Dean and Alece wanted to replicate a sense of celebration in a small and portable form—the donut—that created a feeling of festivity from the look alone.

They began with four flavors—chocolate, strawberry, key lime, and nutmeg, Dean's favorite spice. On any given day there are now more than two dozen flavors, each one more beautiful than the next.

"Decorating takes time; you can't rush it," says Dean. "We don't just smear a lump of frosting on the donut and add some sprinkles." Not only are all the frostings made from scratch, but the decorations are also, including the coconut and nuts toasted every day to retain crispness and freshness. The shops' top flavor is maple bacon, with the bacon caramelized before snippets are placed atop the curlicues of maple frosting. But not far behind it are

German chocolate, with caramel topping, toasted coconut, and chocolate; and cookies and cream, with dabs of white frosting atop the chocolate and half a cookie inserted vertically into the center.

In addition to the retail business, the shops cater many weddings, birthday parties (at which the donuts are stacked in a cake shape), and office parties. "We want to make people happy and let them celebrate the small moments of life, or maybe one of our donuts is a reason to celebrate that day," says pastry chef Alece.

There are three Beyond Glaze shops in Utah. All of them open early, and all are closed on Sunday.

COWBOY DONUTS

ROCK SPRINGS, WYOMING

Every business starts somewhere, and Cowboy Donuts began in owner Jay Hammond's garage, where he and his partner (also his son-in-law), Derek Johnson, used a propane turkey fryer to experiment with donuts made from a recipe culled from the Internet. That was in 2010, and the "cottage" industry became a real business with professional equipment in March 2011.

The last "made fresh daily" donut shop in this southern Wyoming town of 25,000 had closed by the time Jay moved to the region in 2006, and Jay really missed having one available. His father, Don Hammond, had taken Jay and his six siblings to shops all around southern Texas when they were children.

While there are enough cowboys in Wyoming to justify the shop's name, it really comes from these childhood forays. The walls are decorated with cowboy memorabilia and colorful paintings that support the shop's motto: "Dang good donut!"

Cowboy Donuts
1573 Dewar Drive
Rock Springs, Wyoming 82901
(307) 362-3400

www.cowboydonuts.com

Eleven workers arrive at the shop at 2:00 a.m. to start daily production, and by the time they unlock the front door three hours later, the case has been filled. Such stalwarts as traditional yeast-raised glazed donuts are joined by a panoply of both yeast-raised and cake donuts with various fillings and toppings. These include blueberry, devil's food cake with a German chocolate frosting, and traditional buttermilk cake donuts scented with nutmeg.

Derek is very proud of the apple fritters, which are a favorite of locals, as well as the cinnamon buns. "The buns are nice and light and airy, with just the right combination of texture and flavor," he says.

Jay and Derek have devised their donuts for a crowd. In 2013 the pair appeared on *Donut Showdown*, a series produced by the Canadian Food Network, on which three teams of North American donut chefs prepare their specialties. Pitted against two professional pastry chefs from Toronto with a combined thirty years of experience, the pair came in second with the Chocolate Turtle Donut, chocolate donuts with dark chocolate icing spiked with cinnamon and topped with candied pecans and a caramel drizzle.

But the offerings don't stop with donuts. Every day Cowboy Donuts pays homage to its Texan roots with batches of kolaches. These traditional Czech pastries—both sweet and savory—have a long history and enduring popularity in the Lone Star State.

A benefit of kolaches is that the fillings are totally contained in the dough, which makes them easy to eat on the run. Cowboy Donuts features them stuffed with ham and cheese or sausage and cheese, with jalapeño chiles optional. They also do a large version in which the dough encloses a long smoked Polish sausage. The pastries are crafted from slightly sweet buttery yeast dough, and they are baked rather than fried.

Derek, who is finishing his MBA studies, just invented a machine that he believes will be "game changing" for bakers around the country. It allows the dough for kolaches to be rolled mechanically. "A good baker can roll about ninety kolaches an hour, and the machine can do 4,800," he says. Derek's invention emerged victorious from a group of 140 inventors, and he won $40,000 to move his prototype machine to full production.

But there's no automation in the works for the donuts. They'll still be formed and fried up by hand each morning.

APPLE FRITTERS

Makes 15 to 20, depending on size

DOUGH

1 (¼-ounce) package active dry yeast

⅔ cup whole milk, heated to 110°F to 115°F

3½ cups all-purpose flour, divided, plus more for dusting

1 large egg, at room temperature

2 large egg yolks, at room temperature

½ cup apple butter

3 tablespoons unsalted butter, melted and cooled

½ teaspoon apple pie spice

½ teaspoon salt

Vegetable oil for frying

APPLE FILLING

2 tablespoons unsalted butter

4 Granny Smith apples, peeled, cored, and cut into small dice

¼ cup firmly packed light brown sugar

1 teaspoon apple pie spice

½ cup apple cider

2 teaspoons freshly squeezed lemon juice

GLAZE

1 cup apple cider

1 (2-inch) cinnamon stick

1 tablespoon light corn syrup

Pinch of salt

2 cups confectioners' sugar

FRUIT FRITTERS aren't supposed to be pretty. They're supposed to have an irregular, gnarled shape with lots of bumps from the fruit inside of them. To form them, you chop dough that's been layered with the apples into small pieces and then plunk haphazard piles of it in the oil. But there's no wrong way to do it, and making messy things can be fun, especially when they're delicious.

For the dough, combine the yeast, milk, and ½ cup flour in the bowl of a stand mixer fitted with the paddle attachment, and mix well. Set aside for about 10 minutes while the yeast proofs.

When the yeast looks frothy, add the egg, egg yolks, apple butter, butter, apple pie spice, and salt. Beat at medium speed to combine. Add the remaining flour, and beat at low speed until the flour is incorporated, forming a soft dough.

Place the dough hook on the mixer, and knead the dough at medium speed for 2 minutes. Raise the speed to high, and knead for an additional 3 to 4 minutes, or until the dough forms a soft ball and is springy. (If kneading by hand, this will take about 10 to 12 minutes.)

Lightly grease the inside of a large mixing bowl with softened butter or vegetable oil. Add the dough, turning it so it is lightly greased all over. Cover the bowl loosely with a sheet of oiled plastic wrap or a damp tea towel, and place it in a warm, draft-free spot. Allow the dough to rise for 1 to 2 hours, or until it has doubled in bulk.

While the dough rises, prepare the filling. Heat the butter in a large skillet over medium heat. Add the apples and cook, stirring frequently, for 2 minutes. Stir in the brown sugar, apple pie spice, cider, and lemon juice. Cook over medium heat, stirring frequently, for 5 to 10 minutes, or until the apples are tender and the liquid has evaporated. Spread the apples out on a baking sheet to cool completely.

Scrape the dough, which will be sticky, onto a heavily floured surface and with floured hands pat it into a square that is 1 inch thick.

(recipe continues)

Spread half the apples over half the dough, and fold the other half of the dough over it. Fold the package into thirds as you would a letter, and then press it back into a square. Spread the remaining apples on top, and repeat the folding process. Press the dough into a rectangle that is ¾ inch thick.

Use a pizza wheel or sharp serrated knife to cut the dough into 1-inch squares. To form a fritter, gather enough pieces to fill the palm of your hand and place in an irregular mound on a baking sheet lined with a sheet of parchment paper or a silicone baking mat. Repeat until all the dough is used.

Cover the baking sheet with a sheet of oiled plastic wrap, and let the fritters rise in a warm place until doubled in bulk, about 30 to 40 minutes.

While the fritters rise, prepare the glaze. Combine the apple cider and cinnamon stick in a saucepan and bring to a boil over medium-high heat. Lower the heat to medium and reduce the mixture until just ⅓ cup remains. Remove and discard the cinnamon stick, and stir in the corn syrup and salt. Slowly whisk in the confectioners' sugar and beat until smooth. Scrape the glaze into a mixing bowl, and press a sheet of plastic wrap directly into the surface to keep it from hardening.

Heat at least 2 inches of oil to a temperature of 350°F in a Dutch oven or deep skillet. Place a few layers of paper towels on a baking sheet and top it with a wire cooling rack.

Carefully slide a few fritters into the hot oil, being careful not to crowd the pan and making sure that the fritters do not touch each other. Once the fritters float to the top of the oil, fry them for 1 to 1½ minutes, depending on size. Gently flip them over using a wire mesh spoon and fry for an additional 1½ to 2 minutes, or until evenly browned.

Drain the fritters on the rack, blotting them gently with additional paper towels. Fry the remaining fritters in the same manner. While the fritters are still warm, dip the tops into the glaze, turning to coat them well. Place them with the glazed side up on a wire rack set over a sheet of waxed paper. Let the fritters stand for 20 minutes, or until the glaze is set.

The assembled fritters can be refrigerated for up to 4 hours rather than rising at room temperature. Fry them just prior to serving.

GURU DONUTS

A guru is a spiritual teacher, and since February 2013 Guru Donuts has been teaching the people of Boise what artisanal donuts are all about. The donuts are well known in this city of 200,000 because Guru wholesales them to numerous coffee shops as well as participating in the Boise Farmers Market. In June 2014, they opened a retail store in conjunction with Boise Fry Company, another firm that uses a lot of oil.

Before there was a full-time brick-and-mortar shop across from the state capitol building, customers flocked to different parts of the city to savor such Guru creations as the Hipsterberry, with a vivid purple glaze of wild berries scented with lavender, or the Jelly Lama, which marries raspberries, lemon, and thyme in the glaze. The Bart Simpson pays homage to the cartoon character's love of Butterfinger bars with crushed candy adhered to the thick chocolate glaze. Many of the most popular donuts, including the original glazed and the mint chocolate chip, are also available as vegan creations. Special donuts rotate on and off the menu, and include such crowd-pleasers as Lemon Meringue and Banana Cream Pie.

Guru is famous for its savory donuts as well. The shop adds jalapeños and roasted chiles to its dough and tops it with maple and bacon or a Hawaii *kalua* pig creation. In addition to donuts, Guru makes bars, fritters, and twists. Some of the most popular flavors are the Pumpkin-Spiced Chai Fritter and the Adam & Eve, a caramel apple fritter.

Kevin Moran, who owns Guru Donuts with his wife, Angel, and friend, Michael Baker, says he "grew up in a donut culture" in southern California. One of his grandfathers owned a Winchell's Donut House and the other grandfather took him on weekend junkyard treasure hunts that always ended with a stop for donuts. And while Kevin appreciated the aesthetic pleasures of donuts, Michael literally grew up in a Colorado donut shop owned by his parents and knew how to make the sweets.

It seemed like a good omen when the group found a donut fryer listed on Craigslist in 2012, and the Morans were living in a converted 1903 market building that still contained the two original kitchen areas. They turned the downstairs former butcher shop into a donut laboratory and the three of them went to work.

Their first foray was into selling donuts from their home, or as they referred to it, "a donut speakeasy." A few months later, they moved to a commercial kitchen space to increase production, and began selling donuts to the public at a pop-up location on Friday and Saturday mornings, as well as taking part in the farmers' market. Their participation in the market is reflected in their offerings—they buy and use the other vendors' products, such as eggs and homemade jam.

They're now tinkering with a new recipe that would surely reflect the shop's location: a potato donut.

Guru Donuts
204 North Capitol Boulevard
Boise, Idaho 83702
(208) 571-7792

www.gurudonuts.com

TREASURE STATE DONUTS

★   MISSOULA, MONTANA   ★

"Total immersion" is the way that Stephanie Lubrecht, a 25-year-old native of this city of 70,000 in western Montana describes her transformation from pizza chef to donut diva. For the three months of the winter of 2013 she worked by herself from dawn to dusk making donuts in what would become the kitchen of Treasure State Donuts, the only dedicated donut shop in town.

When the shop opened in April 2013 in a space that, for twenty-six years, had been a casual diner near the University of Montana's main campus, Stephanie had worked for three months on tweaking the three basic recipes that she now flavors, fills, and frosts in myriad ways. All of the ancillary products, as well as the donuts themselves, are made daily in the kitchen.

The daily changing menu comprises cake and yeast donuts, and within the classic forms of fritters and jelly donuts, rings and long johns, she blends old-fashioned favorites and contemporary creations.

On the old-fashioned side of her offerings, Boston cream donuts, cinnamon sugar cake donuts, sour cream donuts, and jelly donuts filled with preserves she makes from local fruit, are always on the menu. And then there are her daily dishes. These usually include some sort of fruit fritter, a bacon maple bar (with bacon candied using organic local honey), espresso chip cake donuts, and raised donuts combining homemade Nutella with some sort of fruit and jam. Treasure State

Treasure State Donuts
400 East Broadway Street
Missoula, Montana 59802
(406) 541-0002

www.treasurestatedonuts.com

Donuts also infuses spice blends like chai and aromatic lemon zest into its cake donut dough. Stephanie has recently begun making a few gluten-free options, too.

What unites the offerings is the reliance on purchasing as much as possible from the farmers in the region. "Missoula is very involved in the locavore movement and we source ingredients from the cooperative whenever possible," she says. Another local aspect of the shop is that all the coffee sold with the donuts comes from the Black Coffee Roasting Company (established 2010), the only 100 percent organic coffee roaster in the state.

Erin McEwen, whose family has been running restaurants in Missoula since the 1970s, and her husband, Dmitri Murfin, own Treasure State Donuts. The couple also own The Bridge Pizza, an innovative pizza restaurant where Stephanie worked for six years in both the front and back of the house.

Even though she is only a few credits shy of earning her degree in biology at the University of Montana, Stephanie is happy she took this hiatus to make Treasure State Donuts an exciting place. She posts the daily offerings on Facebook shortly after the shop opens at 6:00 a.m. While she has never been to culinary school, her background in science led her to investigations of the chemistry of food in general and specifically into donuts.

"I've loved baking since I was little, and it's something I wished for years that I could turn into a career, so I'm just glad it's become more than a pipe-dream," she says. And her customers agree.

WASHINGTON

12

10 · 11

11

OREGON

CALIFORNIA

5 · 6 · 7 · 8

9

2 · 3 · 4

1

HAWAII

13

14

Chapter 6

THE PACIFIC STATES

Alice Waters established a beachhead for innovative food when she opened Chez Panisse in Berkeley in 1971, and nearly a half century later, the Left Coast had become the country's leading culinary region. That commitment to quality and innovation is reflected in the donut shops you'll find on the Pacific Coast today. From the Mexican border to the Canadian border, wonderfully original shops are making a wide range of delicious donuts.

Hawaii is also part of this region, and that's where we find a donut of different sorts in both form and flavor. The malasada, a Portuguese donut that arrived with pineapple-plantation workers in the nineteenth-century, while made in a few other states, is the primary donut of the islands.

SIDECAR DOUGHNUTS & COFFEE

Unlike chefs who hear the siren song that lures them to the kitchen during their youth, Brooke Des Prez was in her forties when she decided food was her calling and donuts her passion. This Orange County native is now making her hometown a sweeter place as the chef and co-owner of Sidecar Doughnuts & Coffee.

"Donuts are for everyone, rich and poor, young and old, conservative or liberal," she says. She started catering seven years before the shop opened in the spring of 2013. She conceptualized Sidecar Doughnuts with close friends who became her business partners, Chi-lin and Sumter Pendergrast, and Brooke and Chi-lin began testing donuts on friends and neighbors.

While her roster of donuts changes every month to take advantage of the seasonality of local fruits, some customer favorites remain on the menu. One of these is a huckleberry cake donut with bits of the wild fruit in the donut and a vividly colored glaze on top.

After cooking her way through Thomas Keller's *French Laundry Cookbook,* Brooke committed to using brown butter in any way she can. The Butter and Salt donut, for example, has brown butter in the donut and forms the basis of the glaze; it is finished with a sprinkling of *fleur de sel.* Another brown butter donut contains cornmeal and bits of fresh corn. Almond meal is another signature addition to Brooke's donut recipes.

In addition to a range of yeast-raised and cake donuts, Sidecar Doughnuts also makes Hawaiian malasadas. The filling changes frequently. One month it will be *haupia,* Hawaiian coconut cream, and the next month it might be homemade plum jam or lemon curd.

The shop is decorated with vintage or vintage-inspired artifacts, including an old Victrola. And there are batches of donuts in the fryers from the time the shop opens in the early morning until it closes in the late afternoon. "I think donuts are really best right out of the fryer, and people will wait for a hot batch most of the time," Brooke says.

Not all the donuts are designed to appeal to a customer's sweet tooth. The Green Eggs & Ham remains a star on the menu. Brooke wraps a poached egg in sliced ham and then coats the fragile package in basil hollandaise sauce before frying it up in the only slightly sweet malasada dough. This breakfast donut is only made until 11:00 a.m., but there are other savory options—like a crab salad donut—on the menu occasionally.

There is a gluten-free donut made every day on a weekly cycle, and on Thursdays the case also contains a vegan option. The coffee poured at the shop is Stumptown, a legendary Oregon roaster with shops in Portland, Los Angeles, Seattle, and New York. Both donuts and coffee are also served from the shop's food truck at events.

While news of the wonders of Sidecar's donuts has brought customers from nearby Los Angeles since the shop opened, they will no longer have to trek to the freeway. Sidecar Doughnuts & Coffee will be opening a second location in Santa Monica in the spring of 2015.

Sidecar Doughnuts & Coffee
270 East 17th Street
Costa Mesa, California 92627
(949) 887-2910

Upcoming shop: 631 Wilshire Boulevard
Santa Monica, California 90401

LEMON-GLAZED BLUEBERRY DONUTS

Makes 12

DONUTS

1 cup fresh blueberries

⅓ cup blueberry jam

4 cups bread flour, plus more for dusting

1 tablespoon baking powder

½ teaspoon salt

½ teaspoon ground ginger

½ cup granulated sugar

4 tablespoons (½ stick) unsalted butter, melted and cooled

1 cup whole milk

1 large egg, beaten

Vegetable oil for frying

GLAZE

2 cups confectioners' sugar

1 tablespoon light corn syrup

2 teaspoons grated lemon zest

3 tablespoons freshly squeezed lemon juice

Pinch of salt

WHILE SIDECAR DOUGHNUTS' chef Brooke Des Prez has access to succulent wild huckleberries from the Northwest to use in her donuts, the rest of the country at least has fresh blueberries available. I love the combination of blueberry with lemon, so I joined those two as a donut and glaze.

Combine the blueberries and jam in a food processor fitted with the steel blade. Chop very finely using on-and-off pulsing, but be careful not to purée them.

Combine the flour, baking powder, salt, ginger, and sugar in a mixing bowl and whisk well. Combine the blueberry mixture, butter, milk, and egg in the bowl of a stand mixer fitted with the paddle attachment and beat well at medium speed.

Add the dry ingredients to the wet ingredients, and beat at medium speed to mix well. Scrape the dough onto a sheet of floured plastic wrap and pat it into a circle that is 1 inch thick. Refrigerate the dough for at least 2 hours, or up to 24 hours.

While the dough chills, prepare the glaze. Combine the confectioners' sugar, corn syrup, lemon zest, lemon juice, and salt in a mixing bowl and whisk until smooth. Press a sheet of plastic wrap directly into the surface to keep it from hardening.

Heat at least 2 inches of oil to a temperature of 360°F in a Dutch oven or deep skillet. Place a few layers of paper towels on a baking sheet and top it with a wire cooling rack.

While the oil heats, dust a surface and rolling pin with flour. Roll the chilled dough to a thickness of ½ inch. Use a donut cutter dipped in flour to cut out as many donuts as possible; alternatively, use a 2½-inch cookie cutter and then cut out holes with a ½-inch cutter. Transfer the donuts and holes carefully to a baking sheet sprinkled with flour. Reroll the scraps one time to a thickness of ½ inch and cut out more donuts and holes.

Carefully slide a few donuts into the hot oil, being careful not to crowd the pan and making sure that the donuts do not touch each other. Once the donuts float to the top of the oil, fry them for 1 to 1½ minutes per side, or until evenly browned.

Drain the donuts on the rack, blotting them gently with additional paper towels. Fry the remaining donuts and the donut holes in the same manner. While the donuts are still warm, dip the tops into the glaze, turning to coat them well. Place them with the glazed side up on a wire rack set over a sheet of waxed paper. Let the donuts stand for 20 minutes, or until the glaze is set.

The donuts can be cut out and refrigerated for up to 1 day, lightly covered with plastic wrap. They should not be fried or glazed more than 6 hours prior to serving.

DONUTS HAVE A CAMBODIAN CONNECTION IN SOUTHERN CALIFORNIA

For many Cambodian refugees who, fleeing the brutality of the Khmer Rouge, arrived in the United States in the late 1970s, their English vocabulary almost immediately included words like "glazed," "old-fashioned," and "jelly."

Back in the mid-1990s Cambodians ran more than three-quarters of the donut shops in Southern California. The small independent shops had virtually pushed out Winchell's as the region's leading donut provider. From more than 1,000 shops, the chain declined to about 100 in the 1980s.

Almost half of the 200,000 Cambodians seeking asylum settled in Southern California; one neighborhood of Long Beach was dubbed "Little Phnom Penh." The impetus for their entry into donuts can be traced to one man—Ted Ngoy. He was trained at Winchell's, and he aggregated his own fortune by starting small donut shops. He then sold these shops to new arrivals, with easy credit terms, and trained the newcomers in how to make donuts. Another immigrant sold them the equipment once the training process was over. These donut shops were truly a family business, with the husband and wife working seven days a week and the children working after school and on weekends. As children grew older, they learned how to make the donuts as well as sell them.

These donut shops, like the Chinese laundries a century before, were a way for thousands of Asian immigrants to jump-start their American dreams. But rents in California continued to rise, and many of the donut shops had to expand their offerings to remain viable. By the early 2000s, many of the shops had morphed into outlets for the unlikely combination of donuts and Asian food.

In the Bay Area as well as Southern California, hot food options, many purchased fully cooked from wholesalers, were added to menus to increase the size of the potential market and number of occasions the venue was visited. From Mom's Donuts and Chinese Food to Go in the Silver Lake neighborhood of Los Angeles to Chinese Food & Donuts in the Mission district of San Francisco this "odd couple" of the culinary world thrives today. And many reviews mention that there is excellent fried chicken, too. I guess Federal Donuts in Philadelphia (page 84) doesn't have exclusivity on that combo.

FONUTS

The typical diet in southern California is probably healthier than that in most parts of the country, so it would make sense that a quintessentially indulgent treat like a donut magically turned low-fat would be a runaway success here. But there's no magic wand involved in the success of Fonuts, whose name is a contraction of "faux donuts." Instead there's a pair of bakers who have developed donuts, many of which are gluten-free and vegan, too, that are baked or steamed rather than fried.

Some of the gluten-free and vegan flavors that have captured fans since the shop opened in August 2011 include coconut passion fruit, banana cinnamon, vanilla latte, and peanut butter chocolate. Other combinations (not formulated to fit a specific health or diet profile) are strawberry buttermilk, blueberry Earl Grey, salted caramel, and red velvet.

The case is divided about evenly between the gluten-free and vegan choices and the conventional formulations. It's also divided—as in any donut shop—between yeast-raised donuts and cake donuts.

The concept for Fonuts was the brainchild of voice actor and amateur baker Nancy Truman. Nancy was gluten-intolerant and she began experimenting with baking because she found commercially available gluten-free products to be mediocre in flavor and quality. She ended up selling at the Mar Vista Farmers' Market and rather than

Fonuts
8104 West 3rd Street
Los Angeles, California 90048
(323) 592-3075

www.fonuts.com

baking her gluten-free breads in loaves, she baked them in donut pans.

But what transformed a hobby into a business was when Nancy partnered with one of Los Angeles' most celebrated pastry chefs, Waylynn Lucas. The two met at a local dog park, and Nancy would exercise Waylynn's dog during her herculean shifts in restaurant kitchens.

Waylynn was the executive pastry chef for famed Spanish chef José Andrés at The Bazaar in Beverly Hills, where she created everything from updated versions of José's mother's flan to a coconut floating island that was delivered to diners within a cloud of evaporating liquid nitrogen. She was also pastry chef at legendary chef Joachim Splichal's Patina.

Waylynn says developing yeast-raised donuts that "didn't come out tasting like a loaf of bread" was one of the biggest challenges she's faced. Her answer is her top-secret process of steaming the donuts briefly before baking them. In addition to the donuts sold in large sizes, she also bakes up some mini-donuts each day "to let people try a lot of the flavors at once."

And not all the donuts in the case are sweet. Two savory flavors—Cheddar chorizo and rosemary olive oil—have become signature items. "Donut dough itself is not inherently sweet, what pushes donuts in that direction are the glazes and fillings," says Waylynn. She says that while the sweet donuts sell best in the mornings, the savory ones are very popular later in the day. Bridging the gap is her version of the maple bacon donut.

Waylynn's name is now known for her work out front on television as well as behind the scenes in a restaurant kitchen. In the fall of 2013 she was one of the five female Los Angeles culinary professionals who were part of Bravo's reality show *Eat Drink Love*. One critic described it as "Real Housewives meets Top Chef."

Then in July 2014, she took on the role of mentor to fledgling chefs competing for investment funds from chef Tim Love and restaurateur Joe Bastianich on the CNBC reality show Restaurant Startup. "I can really relate to what these chefs are feeling," says Waylynn. "I left my high-paying job to go back to the basics with Fonuts because I felt so passionately about the concept, so I know how they feel competing for funds."

FONUTS' STRAWBERRY-BUTTERMILK DONUT

Makes 18

THIS IS A CLASSIC recipe at Fonuts, made with fresh strawberries dotting the baked dough and tinting the glaze.

1¼ cups all-purpose flour

¾ cup sugar

½ teaspoon baking soda

Pinch of salt

⅔ cup canola oil

½ cup buttermilk

1 large egg, at room temperature

½ teaspoon distilled white vinegar

½ teaspoon pure vanilla extract

½ cup finely chopped fresh strawberries, divided

2 cups confectioners' sugar

Preheat the oven to 350°F and grease a 6-ring donut pan with oil.

Combine the flour, sugar, baking soda, and salt in a mixing bowl and whisk well. Combine the oil, buttermilk, egg, vinegar, and vanilla in another mixing bowl and whisk until smooth. Pour the liquid ingredients into the dry ingredients and whisk until smooth. Stir in half the strawberries.

Spoon 2 tablespoons of batter into each donut ring and spread it evenly. Bake the donuts in the center of the oven for 13 to 15 minutes, or until a toothpick in the center comes out clean. Cool the donuts on a wire rack, and repeat with the remaining batter.

Purée the remaining strawberries in a blender or a food processor fitted with the steel blade. Scrape the purée into a mixing bowl and stir in the confectioners' sugar. When the donuts are completely cool, dip the tops into the glaze and then set them back on the wire rack for 20 minutes, or until the glaze hardens.

The donuts can be made up to 1 day in advance and kept at room temperature, tightly covered with plastic wrap.

VARIATIONS: Raspberries or blackberries can be substituted for the strawberries.

THE DONUT MAN

Considering the traffic in Los Angeles at all hours of the day and night, the thirty-mile trip from downtown to the city of Glendora in the San Gabriel Valley can take more than an hour. But Angelenos have been making the trek for more than thirty years for the confections prepared twenty-four hours a day, seven days a week at Jim Nakano's Donut Man.

While many shops have limited hours or close when they finish selling that morning's production, that doesn't happen at the Donut Man. The sweet smell coming from the fryer permeates the air around the clock. "We always try to have hot donuts," says Jim, who owns the shop with his wife, Miyoko.

The couple opened the shop in 1972 as a franchise of Foster's Donuts, but then decided they wanted to move in a direction of their own. The Donut Man was born in 1980. The name of the shop came from a chance encounter that Jim and Miyoko had while out for dinner. A young girl recognized him from Foster's Donuts and said "Hello, donut man." It stuck.

In 1974, before he even owned the business, Jim introduced what is now his signature product—a yeast-raised donut filled to the brim with fresh strawberries. The berries are delivered daily from a local farm, and the donuts are sliced almost in half to enclose the generous helping of filling. Those star on the menu from February to June, and when they go out of season, equally juicy and luscious peaches replace them. Jim tells his customers to eat them as you would an overstuffed hamburger, but he also gives out plastic forks.

The strawberry donut is more than a trademark for the Donut Man. In 2013 it was chosen as *the* iconic food of Los Angeles by the viewers of KCET, the public television station, in a bracket competition worthy of the NCAA. It beat out such legendary foods as the cheeseburgers at In-N-Out, the French dip sandwiches at Philippe the Original, and the barbecued chicken pizza at California Pizza Kitchen.

The other donut everyone associates with the Donut Man is the Tiger Tail, which is a braid of glazed chocolate and vanilla dough that could easily feed four people and is so long that it can barely fit into the donut box.

All of the yeast-raised donuts, which compose the majority of the very long menu, are made with potato flour. The options include everything from long johns filled with sweetened cream cheese or fresh fruit to traditionally shaped donuts topped with different flavors of icing. The simple donuts remain less than one dollar, with only the strawberry and peach donuts costing three dollars.

The Donut Man
915 East Route 66
Glendora, CA 91740
(626) 335-9111

www.thedonutmanca.com

The yeast-raised column alone is longer than the options at most donut shops, but that's hardly all the choices. There are old-fashioned donuts done as both buttermilk bars and with chocolate added to the batter, and there is a full range of French crullers, some glazed and others sliced in half and filled with Bavarian cream or other custards.

There's no seating at the Donut Man; customers are served at a walk-up window and there are a few benches. But people still linger in the parking lot chatting because very few would want to drive while tackling one of Jim's donuts.

The Donut Man has been featured on countless television segments, and Jim is now a local celebrity. For this third-generation Japanese American it's a sharp contrast with his childhood, some of which was spent in an internment camp in Arizona during World War II. Though he was stationed in Japan after joining the navy, he met his Japanese wife, Miyoko, while traveling in Europe. He didn't speak any Japanese, but her fluency in English launched the relationship.

Miyoko urged Jim to start the Donut Man, too. It was the second way she changed his life.

The Nickel Diner occupies a space that was another diner in the 1940s, and part of the decor is a series of hand-painted wall menus with the prices of that era. The food options at the current incarnation haven't changed much from what was offered then—including a roster of homemade donuts.

The Nickel Diner is the creation of chef Monica May and her partner in business and in life, Kristen Trattner, who is responsible for the zany interior design. There are mannequin heads representing characters from TV personality Guy Fieri to Marie Antoinette with meringue for their hair in the windows, and floor lamps turned upside down become chandeliers. Describing the pair's contributions, Monica explains, "It's as if she's holding you on her lap and I'm feeding you."

The two owned Banquette, a small sandwich shop that didn't have a kitchen, before launching Nickel Diner in 2008. "I was longing to create food that I couldn't get anywhere else downtown because there weren't any restaurants," says Monica. She knew she wanted to make French toast out of homemade brioche, and soon after mastering that dough she transformed it into the donut dough from which all the diner's donuts are made.

While admitting that she wasn't the first to do a maple bacon donut, Monica thinks she took it to a higher level, and it remains the most popular donut on the menu. "I have more of a savory palate than a sweet palate, and I thought about how won-

Nickel Diner
524 South Main Street
Los Angeles, California 90013
(213) 623-8301

www.nickeldiner.com

derful it was when eating pancakes and maple syrup when some of the syrup dribbled onto the bacon," she says. "That was my inspiration."

Other popular donuts are the Strawberry Almond Crumble, topped with a crumb made from shortbread cookies blended with dried strawberries; the Nutella Donut, dipped in thick chocolate ganache and sprinkled with chopped hazelnut praline; and the Car Bomb. This confection is filled with pastry cream spiked with Jameson Irish whiskey, coated with a glaze made from reduced Guinness stout, and topped with cake crumbs flavored with Guinness, lots of ginger, and other spices.

Two other favorites are the red velvet donut, filled with cream cheese frosting and topped with housemade red velvet cake crumbs, and a chocolate donut coated with ganache and topped with crunchy Valrhona "pearls."

Monica usually sends donut holes to the table as an *amuse-bouche* so diners can contemplate their dessert while eating the meal. The Nickel Diner serves breakfast, lunch, and dinner. What unites the menu is a dedication to top-quality ingredients served as updated comfort food.

While the extensive breakfast menu includes all the traditional favorites, there are also dishes like the Hangover Helper, comprising scrambled eggs with bacon, Italian sausage, and potatoes topped with jalapeño Jack cheese, avocado, and salsa. Another breakfast special is the 5th and Main, named for the diner's location. It is a spicy barbecued pork hash topped with poached eggs.

Specialties on the lunch and dinner menus include Nickel's version of mac and cheese as well as Monica's chicken pozole soup. Other good choices are chicken with mushroom duxelles stuffed under the skin, resting on a bed of old-fashioned hazelnut stuffing; pan-roasted salmon with roasted red pepper sauce, served over buttermilk mashed potatoes; and grilled flatiron steak with chimichurri sauce on a bed of arugula with tomato and avocado.

In this era of restaurant menus priced like fine wine, there's not an entrée on Nickel Diner's menu that is more than fifteen dollars, and many of them are less than ten.

Monica and Kristen live very close to Nickel Diner, in a neighborhood that by all estimates is on the cusp of Skid Row. It was the backdrop used for filming the movie *The Soloist*, the story of Steve Lopez, a columnist for the *Los Angeles Times*, and the homeless schizophrenic violinist Nathaniel Ayres.

"I have to like the people I feed," says Monica, and her customers vary from cops and workers at City Hall to "loft-dwelling hipsters and Drew Barrymore with her kids on Sunday morning."

DYNAMO DONUT + COFFEE

Dynamo Donuts + Coffee has been setting the standard for sophisticated treats in a city in which sophisticated food has been a hallmark for decades. The words that appear frequently in reviews of the wide range of flavors coming out of the open kitchen in this shop in the vibrant Mission District are "complexly flavored," "enticing," and "exciting."

While myriad donut shops list some variation on maple bacon, at Dynamo it's done with succulent apples sautéed in bacon fat worked into the dough along with bacon. Then the cooked donut is given the maple glaze and topped with additional bacon. While the menu at Dynamo Donuts + Coffee lists about ten options daily, both at the shop and at the kiosk on the Marina that it supplies, this one is always on the menu.

These are truly donuts for adults, and the donuts have received rave reviews since owner Sara Spearin first opened in 2008. What Sara brings to donuts is her carefully honed palate for desserts from her more than twenty years as a pastry chef. Her tenure included stints at such legendary restaurants as Postrio, Stars, Liberty

Café, and Foreign Cinema. She had not really been a donut aficionado, but began experimenting with them while on maternity leave in 2007.

Sara customizes each flavor combination with broad strokes and subtle nuances for each donut. For example, the Lemon Sichuan donut has lemon zest worked into the dough and is filled with lemon curd in a two-layer process akin to forming ravioli before the trip to the fryer. But then comes the offbeat element: very finely ground Sichuan pepper mixed with the confectioners' sugar in the coating.

Many of the donuts include a yin-yang of sweet and savory. Aromatic star anise is added to a rich chocolate glaze, and there is fresh orange zest in the dough of the Caramel de Sel donut, which is enrobed in a thick layer of caramel and then sprinkled with *fleur de sel*.

Herbs and spices not usually found in sweets are an integral part of Sara's arsenal. There is both lemon zest and fresh thyme in the dough of the Lemon Thyme donut, and it's topped with a lemony honey glaze. Cardamom, common in Indian cooking, is added to both the dough and glaze for a donut

Dynamo Donut + Coffee
2760 24th Street
San Francisco, California 94110
(415) 920-1978

Dynamo Donut + Coffee:
Marina Kiosk
110 Yacht Road
San Francisco, California 94123
(415) 920-1978

www.dynamodonut.com

that also contains chopped dried apricots and zesty dried currants.

Sara also offers a full line of gluten-free donuts under the moniker "I'm not a Gluten Donut."

While certainly children find many options to their liking, including Peanut Butter Banana and Carrot Cake, there are a few flavors geared to the older generations. One is named the Bitter Queen: it contains candied grapefruit peel and the glaze is topped with bright red crystals of sugar flavored with Campari.

THE RED VELVET RAGE

From Boston to Boise and from Portland, Maine, to Portland, Oregon, red velvet anything and everything is all the rage. But the exact definition of red velvet and the reasons why it's now invading menus remain somewhat of a mystery.

In the early twentieth century, the names "red velvet" and "devil's food" were used almost interchangeably in identical cake recipes. The hint of red color in both was caused by the interaction of acids such as buttermilk and vinegar with cocoa powder. The name may also have something to do with the fact that brown sugar back then was called "red sugar."

By the 1930s, recipes for red devil's food cake to which red food coloring was added began to appear nationally around the holidays. The claim is that its roots are in the posh dining room of New York's Waldorf Astoria Hotel, where John A. Adams, president of the Adams Extract Company in Austin, Texas, ate the cake and then brought the idea back to his marketing people.

Armed with recipes from the supermarket and a bottle of Mr. Adams's red dye, cooks started winning cooking contests at county and state fairs with red velvet cake, integrating it into the American pantheon of flavors.

Then in 1989, a red velvet cake made an appearance as a groom's cake in the film *Steel Magnolias,* and a few years later, when Magnolia Bakery opened in New York, its popularity reached new heights. But the transformation of red velvet to cult status was caused in 2000 when Raven Dennis III, known to all as Cake Man Raven, opened his shop in Brooklyn and red velvet ruled.

According to the research firm Packaged Facts, in 2009 red velvet represented 1.5 percent of menu items in restaurants, and in 2013 it had catapulted to 4.4 percent. But some mutations are taking hold. Chefs are now trying to rid the products of artificial dyes and achieve a red hue with puréed beets, a natural ingredient that has been used in cakes since World War II.

BRENDA'S FRENCH SOUL FOOD

★ SAN FRANCISCO, CALIFORNIA ★

Y ou can transplant a Louisiana girl from the bayous to the San Francisco Bay, but chances are she'll bring some beignets with her. That's what Brenda Buenviaje did, and her trio of sweet and savory beignets are a signature dish at her small restaurant, Brenda's French Soul Food.

Brenda was born in a suburb of the Crescent City to a Creole-Filipino family, so the fare ranged from gumbo to lumpia. She switched her palette for her palate—after graduating with a degree in art, she became a chef in New Orleans creating the fusion food of her background. She moved to San Francisco in 1997 and landed a job as an executive chef at Oritalia, known for its fusion food, too.

After many accolades in the national media, she decided in 2007 to open her own place, which she runs with her wife, Libby. While "soul food" is usually a description of cooking from the African-American heritage, for Brenda it's food that satisfies the soul, what many people term comfort food.

The menu at Brenda's reads like a list of favorites from the French Quarter. There's chicken, sausage, and okra gumbo served at lunch and dinner, along with chicken étouffée smothered in a spicy tomato sauce. Grits, a perennial Southern favorite, are paired with sautéed shrimp or braised beef.

Breakfast is served at Brenda's French Soul Food until 3:00 p.m., and the breakfast and brunch menus include some of these heartier

Brenda's French Soul Food
652 Polk Street
San Francisco, California 94102
(415) 345-8100

www.frenchsoulfood.com

dishes as well as an array of pancakes and foods off the griddle.

Regardless of the time, beignets are on the menu. The sweet beignets are plain, filled with molten Ghirardelli chocolate, or stuffed with cooked Granny Smith apples sweetened with honey butter. But Brenda also creates a crawfish version flavored with cheddar and scallions and spiced with cayenne that draws raves from diners.

And if diners have any appetite remaining, Brenda serves another classic Creole treat: fried fresh peach pies.

COLIBRÍ CENTRAL MEXICAN BISTRO

 SAN FRANCISCO, CALIFORNIA ★

Colibrí, whose name is the Spanish word for "hummingbird," is a Mexican cantina tucked away in the Theater District near Union Square. And the restaurant itself is partly theater. Black and white Spanish-language movies from the 1940s are played against a wall at the front of the house, and the open kitchen at the rear is like performance art.

The owners, Sylvia and Eduardo Rallo, are from Cuernavaca, a posh village near Mexico City. They wanted to open a restaurant that featured authentic cuisine from the center of the country. The appetizers include such popular favorites as guacamole, which can be personalized to any level of spicing, and *queso fundido,* a dip of molten cheese with mushrooms and chorizo. But then there are more unusual options such as *panuchos de cochinita pibil,* consisting of shredded pork in handmade corn shells with refried black beans and

Colibrí Central Mexican Bistro
438 Geary Street
San Francisco, California 94102
(415) 440-2737

www.calibrimexicanbistro.net

pico de gallo. Entrée options run the gamut from chiles rellenos and flautas to enchiladas and chicken mole.

But when it's time for dessert, the focus is on the Mexican version of a donut—the churro. At Colibrí the churros, filled with hot homemade caramel sauce, are delivered hot from the fryer to diners. Topping them is a generous scoop of dulce de leche ice cream, with a sprinkling of confectioners' sugar on the plate. They are a memorable ending to a meal of authentic family recipes.

DELAROSA

★ **SAN FRANCISCO, CALIFORNIA** ★

Pizza is one of the iconic foods of Southern Italy, and so are *bomboloni,* the Italian version of the donut. So it was only natural that they should share the menu at Delarosa, which opened in the Marina District in 2009.

The restaurant belongs to Ruggero Gadaldi, Deborah Blum, and Adriano Paganini, the trio that opened the very successful Baretta in the Mission District. Both spots feature imaginative cocktails and wonderful pizzas made on ultra-thin crusts, along with an extensive menu of panini, pasta, and salads.

The antipasti selection is long and changes seasonally, taking advantage of the region's heralded small organic farms. The emphasis of the menu is

Delarosa
2175 Chestnut Street
San Francisco, California 94123
(415) 673-7100

www.delarosasf.com

on vegetarian options, along with the addition of some fried seafood and grilled meat skewers.

For donut devotees, the standout dessert at Delarosa is a trio of deep-fried, light and pillowy bomboloni with a trio of dipping sauces. There is a rich dark chocolate, a thick raspberry, and a mascarpone cream sauce. The donuts are delivered hot, and they're coated with sugar.

PSYCHO DONUTS

Real hospital nurses don't wear white uniforms with pert little starched white caps on their heads, but that's the costume donned by the staff of Psycho Donuts. The descriptions of the donuts are scribbled on prescription pads in the case, and customers are handed a small square of bubble wrap to pop to alleviate the anxiety of having to make an ordering decision.

And there is anxiety. Who could easily choose between a Dead Elvis (a cream-filled yeast donut crowned with a combination of banana slices, bacon, peanut butter, and jelly), a Dirty Turtle (a chocolate cake donut with cheesecake frosting, crushed Oreo cookies, and a caramel drizzle), and a Strawberry Margarita (with real tequila in the pastry cream, and topped with strawberry frosting with drizzles of key lime and sea salt)?

Not all the donuts are in uniform shapes, either, although there are many rounds and squares in the bunch. The Comfortably Numb is two pieces joined to look as if a person were wearing a straitjacket dusted with confectioners' sugar, and the Crazy Face is a triangle onto which a maple-filled triangular "nose" is affixed and then a mouth and eyes are painted on. A collection of small rectangles are decorated to resemble a tray of sushi, and a pair of Pocky stick cookies is poised on the plate like chopsticks.

Psycho Donuts, which opened in Campbell in 2009, is the brainchild of former Silicon Valley whiz kid Jordan Zweigoron, a Chicago native who was a business development executive at WebEx

2006 South Winchester Boulevard
Campbell, California 95008
(408) 533-1023

288 South Second Street
San Jose, California 95113
(408) 533-1023

www.psycho-donuts.com

when he launched Psycho. His intention was to create a total sensory experience for customers, not just sell them donuts. He calls the shops "the world's first and only light-hearted asylum for wayward donuts." Not everyone saw the humor in his theme of "bringing out the crazy in all of us." Within two weeks of the opening, mental health groups began boycotting the shop and claiming its theme was offensive and perpetuated stereotypes about mentally ill individuals. The controversy raged for a few months, and Jordan finally removed both the straitjacket and the padded cell from the shop's collection of interior design elements. He also changed the name of the Bipolar Donut to Mood Swing and Massive Head Trauma is now called Headbanger.

The notoriety from the controversy brought in business, however, and a second satellite shop opened in San Jose in 2010. The shops are just a few miles apart and all the donuts for both are made in Campbell and trucked hourly to the second location.

The latest addition to the Psycho Donut family of far-out concepts is the Danolli, which Jordan describes as "a head-on collision between an innocent donut and a cannoli." The body is a cylindrical form filled with the same sort of sweetened ricotta used for the classic Sicilian pastry. It has miniature chocolate chips applied at either end, and the frosted body has crushed crispy cannoli shells applied to the outside.

But it seems that many of the inventions springing from Psycho Donuts lead to press beyond the food pages. To celebrate National Donut Day in 2013, the shops announced that they were giving away Foie Bombs to the first fifty customers. The round donut was filled with foie gras and topped with a fried sage leaf, with a small tube of honey, fig, and balsamic vinegar reduction inserted through it. This was just a year after the sale of foie gras was banned in California, a measure promoted by a consortium of anti–animal cruelty groups. Psycho Donuts responded that it was not selling foie gras, it was giving it away. But the pickets and threats arrived anyway.

FOIE GRAS DONUTS

The French have been serving glasses of Sauternes with foie gras to start a meal for centuries, and it's common to pair the richness of fattened duck or goose liver with sweet fruit preserves. While Psycho Donuts was pushing, if not bending, the laws of California with the Foie Bomb because the sale of foie gras is illegal in that state, there are foie gras donuts alive and well in other parts of the country.

Perhaps the best known of them is at Do or Dine in Brooklyn (1108 Bedford Avenue, Brooklyn, New York, 11216, (718) 684-2290), where chef Justin Warner fills donuts with foie gras and homemade jam. The item is listed under the Small Plates section of his menu.

At JM Curley's in Boston (21 Temple Place, Boston, Massachusetts, 02111, (617) 338-5333), the foie gras is used as a glaze on a donut stuffed with strawberry rhubarb compote and topped with crystals of candied basil. It's listed in the dessert section.

BLUE STAR DONUTS

Restaurateurs Micah Camden and Katie Poppe had an epiphany when they visited St. John Bakery in London three years before opening Blue Star Donuts in December 2012. What they tasted were ethereally light brioche donuts, some filled with pastry cream, others with homemade jams, and some with a mixture of the two. They were like no other donuts, and they are what customers clamor for at the two Blue Star Donuts shops in Portland.

As cooks know, the process of making this rich butter and egg yeast dough is hardly quick; it's a two-day process. In fact, some of us consult actuarial charts before starting a loaf. But Micah and Katie decided it was worth the labor to get the result they'd sampled across the pond.

These are dignified and dapper donuts in traditional shapes, with or without a hole, depending on if they're destined for filling or just glazing. While items on top of the glazes add textural interest, the donuts from Blue Star are praised for

1237 SW Washington Street
Portland, Oregon 97205
(503) 265-8410

3549 SE Hawthorne Street
Portland, Oregon 97214
(503) 477-9635

www.bluestardonuts.com

the flavor combinations of their fillings and glazes. They are, as the motto reads, "Donuts for Grownups."

A signature is the Crème Brûlée donut, the top of which is crispy and caramelized, with a plastic vial of Cointreau sticking into the cream filling. Another donut of note is Blue Star's take on fried chicken and waffles; in their version, nuggets of fried chicken top a donut glazed with spiced honey.

Mixing savory and sweet is a thread through many of the flavors. One that never cycles off the menu is glazed with a combination of blueberry, bourbon, and basil. Other favorites are the coffee and coconut cheesecake, a donut filled with Meyer lemon and key lime curd, and a donut filled with blackberry compote and topped with peanut-butter powder.

Some donut combinations are based on a tropical theme. The dulce de leche is given a crunch with chopped hazelnuts, and another donut sports crushed cacao nibs sprinkled over a passion fruit glaze.

While the majority of the donuts are made from the brioche dough, there are a few exceptions. Blue Star makes old-fashioned buttermilk donuts, too, and one of the most popular is coated with an intensely flavored raspberry glaze. The other exception is a fruit fritter made with organic local fruits, such as cherries, pears, and peaches. The Hard Apple Cider Fritter is a signature item with good reason. The apples are in a fritter batter that is aromatic with spices, and then the glaze is given the same brûlée treatment as the crème brûlée donut.

The dough is made from regional products, such as cage-free eggs from Stiebrs Farms, European-style butter from Larsen's Creamery, organic flour from Shepherds Grain, and whole milk from Sunshine Dairy. The same local sourcing extends to serving Portland's highly touted Stumptown Coffee.

The interior design is quite austere; in fact, it's been compared to an operating room. Most of the walls are covered in shiny white tiles, and the floor-to-ceiling windows allow natural light to pour into the space. And customers can watch donuts being made.

The second shop opened in June 2014, and it has a commissary building in the back to chill a sufficient amount of dough to keep both outlets stocked. "Now both shops will be able to be open later because we were literally restrained by our refrigeration capacity," says Katie. "We call these 'new concept design flaws.'" But from the number of customers clamoring for donuts daily, that's about the only flaw at Blue Star Donuts.

CACAO NIBS

Cacao nibs have become the darlings of desserts in recent years. They're folded into ice creams and cakes or used as a sprinkling on top of a glaze or frosting. What they are is bits of fermented, dried, and roasted cacao beans that have been finely ground. They taste intensely of chocolate, but they haven't been mixed with any sugar, so they're not sweet at all. The texture is crunchy yet tender, and they pair well with savory foods. You can sprinkle them on top of a salad or use them in a crust for baked chicken, especially if served with a mole sauce.

BLUEBERRY BOURBON BASIL GLAZE

Makes 3 cups

1 pint fresh blueberries

¾ cup firmly packed fresh basil leaves

¼ cup bourbon

Pinch of salt

3 to 4 cups confectioners' sugar

THE VIVID PURPLE HUE of this glaze sends a strong fruity message, and that is then tempered by heady bourbon and aromatic basil. It may sound like a strange combination, but once you try it, you'll see why it's a signature at this Portland donut shop.

Combine the blueberries, basil leaves, bourbon, and salt in a blender or food processor fitted with the steel blade. Purée until smooth.

Transfer the mixture to the bowl of a stand mixer fitted with the whisk attachment. Add 3 cups of the sugar and whisk at low speed until blended. Increase the speed to medium and whisk for 2 minutes, or until the glaze is completely smooth. Add additional sugar, a few tablespoons at a time, if the glaze is too thin; the thickness depends on the water content of the blueberries.

The glaze can be made up to 3 hours in advance and kept at room temperature with a sheet of plastic wrap pressed directly into the surface to keep it from hardening.

VOODOO DOUGHNUT

Tres Shannon, who with longtime friend Kenneth "Cat Daddy" Pogson opened their first twenty-four-hour donut shop in 2003, "never thought when I was eighteen that I'd be running the craziest donut shop in the world." But that's what the two now do, and it's four shops rather than one. There's a second in Portland and one in nearby Eugene, and then they crossed into Colorado and opened a shop in Denver.

When you add up their production, it's about twenty tons of dough a week, which is served round the clock to everyone from barflies in the middle of the night to young moms pushing strollers to bike messengers in need of energy in the middle of the afternoon.

In addition to donuts—both vegan and traditional—the duo sell a line of customized clothing and other merchandise bearing the shop's slogan: "The Magic Is in the Hole." In addition to t-shirts in a rainbow of colors for both children and adults, there are trinkets ranging from key chains to necklaces to perpetual candles.

The owners became ordained ministers in the Universal Life Church, which is basically a correspondence course, and more than a hundred legal weddings and non-binding commitment ceremonies take place every year in the stores. Some have bridesmaids, while others are less formal, and all end with munching donuts and sipping coffee. "The most we ever did was eight on one Halloween," says Tres, adding that

22 SW 3rd Avenue
Portland, Oregon 97204
(503) 241-4704

1501 NE Davis Street
Portland, Oregon 97232
(503) 235-2666

20 East Broadway
Eugene, Oregon 97401
(541) 868-8666

1520 East Colfax Avenue
Denver, Colorado 80218
(303) 597-3666

www.voodoodoughnut.com

"people who get married in a donut shop clearly have a sense of whimsy."

While the events like mayoral candidates' donut-eating contests and the weddings keep Voodoo Doughnut in the news, what keeps the lines extending out the door every day are the donuts, both yeast-raised and cake, with a few old-fashioned cakes, too.

There's the signature Voodoo Doll filled with raspberry jelly and sporting a pretzel stake in lieu of a needle. Tres also claims that they were the first to make and popularize the maple bacon donut when they introduced it in 2003. "I describe it as where the meat meets the sweet," says Tres.

The names of the donuts are catchy, and some of the flavor combinations sound as if people under some sort of magical spell created them. The Mango Tango is a yeast-raised donut filled with mango jelly and topped with vanilla frosting and a sprinkling of bright orange Tang. Cayenne mixed into the cinnamon sugar gives the Mexican Hot Chocolate, built on a chocolate cake donut, both meanings of the word "hot."

While many of the donuts are recognizable round donuts, either with or without a hole, others are far more freeform. The Memphis Mafia is a mound of fried dough with banana chunks and cinnamon, covered in a glaze with chocolate frosting, peanut butter, chopped peanuts, and chocolate chips on top. One of the more unusual combinations is the Dirty Snowball: It's a chocolate cake donut with hot pink marshmallow topping, dipped in coconut, with a dollop of peanut butter in the center.

But only couples taking advantage of Voodoo for their wedding get to take bites from the Donut of Love. It's a concoction piled high with sprinkles, chocolate chips, and pretzel sticks.

Not all the donuts on Voodoo's menu are crazy. The timid among the customers can opt for anything from an unadorned vanilla cake donut to one dusted with confectioners' sugar to simple glazed French crullers and jelly donuts. But health officials quickly removed two salubrious options from the menu—the Nyquil Glazed and the Vanilla Pepto Crushed Tums donuts.

There are now four locations of Voodoo Doughnut.

MAPLE BACON DONUTS

Makes 12

DONUTS

1 (¼-ounce) package active dry yeast

¾ cup whole milk, heated to 110°F to 115°F

3 tablespoons granulated sugar

¼ cup lukewarm water

1 large egg, at room temperature

¼ cup bacon grease, melted and cooled (but still liquid)

2 cups bread flour

1 cup all-purpose flour, plus more for dusting

½ teaspoon freshly grated nutmeg

½ teaspoon salt

Vegetable oil for frying

GLAZE AND TOPPING

8 slices bacon

2 tablespoons firmly packed dark brown sugar

⅓ cup pure maple syrup, divided

1 tablespoon light corn syrup

½ teaspoon pure vanilla extract

2 cups confectioners' sugar

MORE THAN HALF of the donut shops and restaurants in this book feature yeast-raised donuts topped with maple glaze with some sort of bacon affixed to it. The bacon—which can be plain or candied and occasionally given some heat from mustard or cayenne—can be in large hunks or small slices. I'm placing this recipe here because Tres Shannon, one of the owners of Voodoo Doughnut, claims to have introduced the now-ubiquitous combination, and due to the opening date of Voodoo, I tend to agree with him. My version uses bacon grease both in the donuts and in the glaze, which I think adds to its harmonious flavor.

Combine the yeast, milk, and sugar in the bowl of a stand mixer fitted with the paddle attachment, and mix well. Set aside for about 10 minutes while the yeast proofs.

When the yeast looks frothy, add the water, egg, and bacon grease and mix well. Add the bread flour, all-purpose flour, nutmeg, and salt, and beat at low speed until flour is incorporated, forming a soft dough.

Place the dough hook on the mixer, and knead the dough at medium speed for 2 minutes. Raise the speed to high, and knead for an additional 3 to 4 minutes, or until the dough forms a soft ball and is springy. (If kneading by hand, this will take about 10 to 12 minutes.)

Lightly grease the inside of a large mixing bowl with softened butter or vegetable oil. Add the dough, turning it so it is lightly greased all over. Cover the bowl loosely with a sheet of oiled plastic wrap or a damp tea towel, and place it in a warm, draft-free spot. Allow the dough to rise for 1 to 2 hours, or until it has doubled in bulk.

While the dough rises, prepare the glaze and topping. Preheat the oven to 375°F. Line a baking sheet with heavy-duty aluminum foil and place a wire rack on top of it.

(recipe continues)

Toss the bacon with the brown sugar and 2 tablespoons of the maple syrup. Coat it evenly and arrange the slices on the wire rack. Bake the strips in the center of the oven for 15 to 20 minutes, or until crisp. Dab the bacon with paper towels while it's hot, but do not drain it on paper towels or it will stick to them. When the bacon is cool and crisp, break it into small pieces, and set aside. Reserve the bacon grease for the glaze.

For the glaze, combine the remaining maple syrup, corn syrup, 1 tablespoon of the reserved bacon grease, and vanilla in a mixing bowl and whisk well. Add the confectioners' sugar and whisk until smooth. Press a sheet of plastic wrap directly into the surface to keep it from hardening.

Line a baking sheet with parchment paper or a silicone baking mat. Punch the dough down. Dust a surface and rolling pin with flour. Roll the dough to a thickness of ½ inch. Use a donut cutter dipped in flour to cut out as many donuts as possible; alternatively, use a 3-inch cookie cutter and then cut out holes with a ¾-inch cutter. Reroll the scraps one time to a thickness of ½ inch and cut out more donuts and holes.

Cover the baking sheet with a sheet of oiled plastic wrap, and let the donuts rise in a warm place until doubled in bulk, about 30 to 40 minutes.

Heat at least 2 inches of oil to a temperature of 365°F in a Dutch oven or deep skillet. Place a few layers of paper towels on a baking sheet and top it with a wire cooling rack.

Carefully slide a few donuts into the hot oil, being careful not to crowd the pan and making sure that the donuts do not touch each other. Once the donuts float to the top of the oil, fry them for 1 minute. Gently flip them over using a wire mesh spoon or a chopstick and fry for an additional 1 minute, or until evenly browned. Drain the donuts on the rack, blotting them gently with additional paper towels. Fry the remaining donuts and the donut holes in the same manner. While the donuts are still warm, dip the tops into the glaze, turning to coat them well. Place them with the glazed side up on a wire rack set over a sheet of waxed paper. Top the glaze with some of the candied bacon. Let the donuts stand for 20 minutes, or until the glaze is set.

The donuts can be cut out and refrigerated for up to 1 day, lightly covered with plastic wrap. They should not be fried or glazed more than 6 hours prior to serving.

TOP POT HAND-FORGED DOUGHNUTS & COFFEE

Brothers Mark and Michael Klebeck were custom woodworkers and building contractors when they turned their minds to donuts. It's now been fourteen years since their first Top Pot Hand-Forged Doughnuts & Coffee location opened in the Capitol Hill area of Seattle, and they now have a chain of shops all through the Puget Sound region, plus a few in other parts of the country. But their sense of pride in the craftsmanship of their work remains strong, as does their allegiance to their Polish grandmother's original donut recipe.

Top Pot's offerings encompass the basic three families of donut—cake, yeast-raised, and old-fashioned—plus fritters. The donuts gain their huge fan base from the inherent flavors of the dough, frostings, and fillings. The presentation of the donuts is straightforward with few fancy flourishes or tricks. They focus on the classics.

"Our old-fashioned donuts with their irregular edges and crisp exterior is perhaps our biggest seller," says Mark. While it's always on the menu, it has seasonal variations, such as pumpkin in the fall. Fritters also change with the season: in early summer they will be dotted with succulent local blueberries, which turn to peaches in August as the crop becomes ripe.

The yeast-raised donuts are filled with everything from jams made from local fruits to lemon curd to Bavarian cream. Top Pot does have its own version of maple bacon; it does make glazes from

The Downtown Seattle Flagship Café
2124 5th Avenue
Seattle, Washington 98121
(206) 728-1966

The Original Shop on Capitol Hill
609 Summit Avenue East
Seattle, Washington 98102
(206) 323-7841

Texas Location
8611 Hillcrest Avenue
Dallas, Texas 75225
(469) 232-9911

www.toppotdoughnuts.com

salted caramel; and one of the signature donuts—a cake donut with pink icing covered with white coconut—is named Feather Boa. But most flavor combinations are very tame.

The name comes from an old neon sign that the two bought from a shuttered Chinese restaurant a few years before they opened. The name was Topspot, but in the intervening time the letter S had fallen off, so what they had was Top Pot. This merging of the old with the new is part of the shops' image. Mark and Michael want customers to linger. The shops have built-in bookcases full of reading material as well as Wi-Fi, and old TV sets and other vintage touches make for a homey decor.

Many of their recipes are also now part of the cookbook they authored with food writer Jess Thomson, *Top Pot Hand-Forged Doughnuts: Secrets and Recipes for the Home Baker*, published by Chronicle Books in 2011.

Top Pot has made a few rather drastic course corrections in the direction the business would take. For five years they were allied with another company based in Seattle—Starbucks. They went from supplying donuts to a few hundred shops in western Washington in 2005 to contracting with bakeries to fill donut cases in fourteen thousand stores worldwide by 2010 when they decided that the relationship was not working for their ultimate goals.

In addition to their own shops, Top Pot now sells its donuts to QFC supermarkets in Washington, and also sells bags of its own roasted coffee beans. Another expansion happened in 2012, when Top Pot introduced a line of ice cream flavors tied to donuts, with such flavors as Maple Bar and Apple Fritter, some of which contain bits of pastry.

They are also planning to expand to the East Coast and possibly into Chicago in the next few years. "We've got a loyal fan base out there, and our inbox is filled with emails asking for us to come to other cities," says Mark.

There are nineteen Top Pot Hand-Forged Doughnuts & Coffee shops in the Seattle and Puget Sound area.

ORANGE-PISTACHIO CAKE DONUTS

Makes 12

Adapted from *Top Pot Hand-Forged Doughnuts* by Mark and Michael Klebeck with Jess Thomson (Chronicle Books, 2011)

MARK AND MICHAEL say you can use this as a master recipe any time you want to contrast citrus flavors and nuts. You might try lemon in place of the orange and almonds instead of pistachio nuts.

DONUTS

3 cups cake flour, plus more for dusting

1 teaspoon baking powder

½ teaspoon salt

2 tablespoons unsalted butter, softened

⅔ cup granulated sugar

1 large egg, at room temperature

1 large egg yolk, at room temperature

1 teaspoon pure vanilla extract

½ teaspoon orange extract

Grated zest from 1 large orange

⅔ cup whole milk

Vegetable oil for frying

1 cup chopped unsalted pistachio nuts

ICING

4½ cups confectioners' sugar

1½ teaspoons light corn syrup

¼ teaspoon salt

¼ teaspoon pure vanilla extract

¼ teaspoon pure orange extract

Grated zest of 1 large orange

⅓ cup freshly squeezed orange juice, plus more if necessary

Combine the flour, baking powder, and salt in a mixing bowl and whisk well. Combine the butter and sugar in the bowl of a stand mixer fitted with the paddle attachment. Beat at low speed until the mixture looks like coarse sand. Add the egg, egg yolk, vanilla, and orange extract, and beat until light and fluffy, scraping the sides of the bowl as necessary. Beat in the orange zest.

Gradually add the dry ingredients to the wet ingredients, alternating with the milk, beating until the flour is just combined. Scrape the dough into the center of a large sheet of floured plastic wrap and pat it into a pancake about 1 inch thick. Refrigerate the dough for at least 1 hour.

While the dough is chilling, make the icing. Combine the confectioners' sugar, corn syrup, salt, vanilla, orange extract, zest, and orange juice in the bowl of a stand mixer fitted with the paddle attachment. Blend at low speed until all the sugar has been incorporated, scraping the sides of the bowl as necessary. If the icing seems too thick, add orange juice 1 teaspoon at a time until thinner. Press a sheet of plastic wrap directly into the surface to keep it from hardening.

Heat at least 2 inches of oil to a temperature of 370°F in a Dutch oven or deep skillet. Place a few layers of paper towels on a baking sheet and top it with a wire cooling rack.

While the oil heats, dust a surface and rolling pin generously with flour. Roll the dough to a thickness of ½ inch. Use a donut cutter dipped in flour to cut out as many donuts as possible; alternatively, use a 3-inch cookie cutter and then cut out holes with a 1-inch cutter.

(recipe continues)

Transfer the donuts and holes carefully to a baking sheet sprinkled with flour. Reroll the scraps one time to a thickness of ½ inch and cut out more donuts and holes.

Carefully slide a few donuts into the hot oil, being careful not to crowd the pan and making sure that the donuts do not touch each other. Once the donuts float to the top of the oil, fry them for 1 minute per side, or until evenly browned.

Drain the donuts on the rack, blotting them gently with additional paper towels. Fry the remaining donuts and the donut holes in the same manner. Allow the donuts to cool completely, then dip the tops into the icing, turning to coat them well. Sprinkle each one with chopped pistachio nuts as soon as it is iced. Place the donuts with the glazed side up on a wire rack set over a sheet of waxed paper. Let the donuts stand for 20 minutes, or until the icing is set.

The donuts can be cut out and refrigerated for up to 1 day, lightly covered with plastic wrap. They should not be fried or iced more than 6 hours prior to serving.

LEONARD'S BAKERY

The nineteenth century was a period when thousands of people moved from one country to another in search of work, and they brought their national foods with them. It was in June 1882 that Arsenio and Amelia DoRego, natives of Portugal's São Miguel Island in the Azores, landed on the Hawaiian island of Maui. They were moving to this foreign territory to work in the sugarcane fields, and they brought with them traditional Portuguese dishes, including the recipe for malasadas, round yeast-raised donuts made without a hole.

In 1915 their grandson Leonard was born, and in 1946, following World War II, Leonard and his wife, Margaret, moved to Honolulu with their young daughter. Six years later, after gaining experience, Leonard founded Leonard's Bakery, which has been run by the family now for sixty-three years, with Leonard III and his brother at the helm.

Malasadas were the traditional sweet served in the Azores on Shrove Tuesday, the day of feasting prior to the start of Lent on Ash Wednesday. Leonard's mother suggested them as a special a few months after the bakery opened in 1952. While the bakers at Leonard's feared they might be too foreign to the islanders, malasadas instantly caught on and became the state's signature donut.

Leonard's Bakery moved into its present space in 1957, and it has not expanded to other storefront locations. However, this third generation of Rego owners expanded the business with food trucks, cooking malasadas to order around the island.

While the form and recipe are Portuguese, Leonard's masaladas are a fusion with Hawaiian flavors. The original form can be dusted with traditional sugar or cinnamon sugar or with powdered *li hing mui,* which is not found outside the state.

Li hing mui is a plum native to Guangdong Province in China, and the powder has a complex profile that combines sweet, sour, and salty tastes. While many people find it strange at first, it's as common in Hawaii as chiles are in Texas. The powder is made from plum skin that was pickled in licorice and then sweetened and salted before grinding. In Hawaii the powder is sprinkled on everything from fruit salad to popcorn and shaved ice, and used, of course, as a coating for malasadas.

Fillings for the malasada puffs also show a Hawaiian influence. In addition to custard, the most popular ones are *haupia,* a pudding made from coconut and coconut milk, and *dobash,* a rich chocolate named for the cake by the same name popular in the islands. Other tropical fruits native to Hawaii, such as a yellow passion fruit called *lilikoi,* are also used as fillings for malasadas as well as traditional tarts.

While malasadas are what put Leonard's Bakery on the map, the shop also makes a full range of donuts and other pastries, as well as sausage rolls. But the second mainstay of the menu remains *pão doce,* a Portuguese sweet bread whose recipe came from the Azores back in the nineteenth century.

Leonard's Bakery
933 Kapahulu Avenue
Honolulu, Hawaii 96816
(808) 737-5591

For the location
of the Malasadamobile,
call (808) 341-2428.

www.leonardshawaii.com

MALASADAS

1 tablespoon active yeast

1 cup light cream, heated to 110°F to 115°F, divided

1½ cups granulated sugar, divided

4 cups bread flour, divided, plus more for dusting

3 large eggs, at room temperature

3 tablespoons unsalted butter, melted and cooled

½ teaspoon freshly grated nutmeg

½ teaspoon salt

Vegetable oil for frying

MALASADAS WERE BORN in Portugal, but an Americanized version is Hawaii's most popular donut. Similar to the beignets of New Orleans, malasadas are made from yeast-raised dough that is fried without a hole, which means they can be stuffed with any manner of jelly or pastry cream.

Combine the yeast, ¾ cup warm cream, ¼ cup of the sugar, and ½ cup of the flour in the bowl of a stand mixer fitted with the paddle attachment, and mix well. Set aside for about 10 minutes while the yeast proofs.

When the yeast looks frothy, add the remaining cream, eggs, melted butter, nutmeg, and salt, and beat well at medium speed. Add ¼ cup of the remaining sugar and the remaining flour, and beat at low speed until the flour is incorporated, forming a soft dough.

Place the dough hook on the mixer, and knead the dough at medium speed for 2 minutes. Raise the speed to high, and knead for an additional 3 to 4 minutes, or until the dough forms a soft ball and is springy. (If kneading by hand, this will take about 10 to 12 minutes.)

Lightly grease the inside of a large mixing bowl with softened butter or vegetable oil. Add the dough, turning it so it is lightly greased all over. Cover the bowl loosely with a sheet of oiled plastic wrap or a damp tea towel, and place it in a warm, draft-free spot. Allow the dough to rise for 1 to 2 hours, or until it has doubled in bulk.

Line a baking sheet with parchment paper or a silicone baking mat. Punch down the dough and divide it into 12 pieces. Form each piece into a ball with greased hands and arrange them on the prepared baking sheet, patting them down lightly. Cover the baking sheet with a sheet of oiled plastic wrap, and let rise in a warm place until doubled in bulk, about 45 minutes.

Place the remaining sugar in a shallow bowl. Heat at least 2 inches of oil to a temperature of 350°F in a Dutch oven or deep skillet. Place a few layers of paper towels on a baking sheet and top it with a wire cooling rack.

Carefully add a few donuts into the hot oil, being careful not to crowd the pan and making sure that the donuts do not touch each other. Cook for 1½ to 2 minutes per side, or until golden brown and puffed. Drain the donuts on the rack, blotting them gently with additional paper towels. Fry the remaining donuts in the same manner. Once the donuts are cool enough to handle, coat them in the bowl of sugar. Serve as soon as possible.

The dough can be refrigerated overnight, with the shaping, second rising, and frying to take place the next day.

VARIATION: Add ¾ to 1 teaspoon ground cinnamon to the sugar used for coating the donuts.

T. KOMODA STORE & BAKERY

MAUI, HAWAII

★

T. Komoda Store & Bakery
3674 Baldwin Avenue
Makawao, Maui, Hawaii 96768

(808) 572-7261

Krispy Kreme has established a beachhead on Maui, but natives and tourists alike pass by its convenient location near the airport to trek sixty miles to the village of Makawao. In the mountains on the way to view sunrise from the top of Mount Haleakala, they can experience a kebab of glazed donuts and malasadas filled with guava at T. Komoda Store & Bakery.

Takezo and Shigeri Komoda started the business as a restaurant in 1916, just after the birth of their son, Takeo, and over the decades the family of six boys and two girls all worked at the counter, feeding cowboys and plantation workers and then the soldiers. Bread was always a staple, and from bread they started making donuts.

The business moved to its current location, a white shop with tropical green trim, in 1945, and now a third and fourth generation are in charge. In addition to the racks of donuts, cream puffs, pies, and cookies, the store offers what you would expect from a small general store in a country village. There are newspapers, canned goods, and even fishing gear.

The kitchen is small, yet more than one hundred gallons of pastry cream a day are produced on a four-burner stove alongside the donut fryers. The entire back wall is an oven that can produce seventy-two dozen cream puff shells at one time.

By far the most popular donut is the one that could feed a family—if they cared to share.

Threaded onto a skewer and then fried are about eight small rounds of yeast-raised dough. The kebabs are then glazed, and they can also be augmented with anything from toasted coconut to chopped macadamia nuts grown in sight of the shop. As on all Hawaiian islands, Portuguese puffs called malasadas reign supreme on Maui. At T. Komoda's they're filled with pastry cream or a combination of pastry cream and jam made from tropical fruits like guava and mango.

The chief baker is now Calvin Shibuya, the husband of Takeo Komoda's granddaughter, Betty. He was an aeronautical engineer in the air force and after retirement traded his uniform for an apron. Now Betty and Calvin's daughter, Michelle, is also part of the team. And a team is what's needed. On busy Saturdays they'll fry up 200 pounds of donut dough, and all the work, as it was in Takeo's day, is done by hand. There is great longevity among the staff; many of the workers are in their seventies and have never worked anywhere else.

SLURP SOME SAIMIN BEFORE YOU DOWN THE DONUTS

When T. Komoda Store & Bakery began in 1916, it was a restaurant, and a dish always on the menu was *saimin*.

There are many similarities across cuisines, especially when it comes to soups loaded up with goodies. In Hawaii, *saimin* is such a fusion food, and it is now recognized as the traditional state dish. The name itself is a compound of two Chinese words meaning "thin" and "noodle."

The soup was developed at the end of the nineteenth century, and it contains elements drawn from the various ethnic cuisines of the workers who populated the islands' pineapple and sugarcane plantations: Chinese, Japanese, Korean, Filipino, Portuguese, and indigenous Hawaiian. The only constants of *saimin* are wheat noodles in a hot *dashi* broth. The additions to that broth then come from all over, as a communal pot was made to feed the laborers.

If there were a number of Portuguese represented in the group, there might be *linguiça* or other sausage added; *dashi* broth and strips of *nori* reflect Japanese influence; and cabbage would be prevalent if the Koreans had any left over from making a batch of *kimchi.* While scallions are traditionally included as a garnish, you may also find chopped bok choy, shredded carrots, slices of roasted pork, and halved hard-cooked eggs. The solid morsels are pulled from the bowl with chopsticks, and then the nutritious broth is slurped in the time-honored fashion.

Saimin is only available in Hawaii, but its fame is national. In 2006, the James Beard Foundation recognized Hamura's Saimin Stand on Kauai with its America's Classic Award for "preserving America's culinary heritage and diversity." Matriarch Aiko Hamura started the restaurant in 1951, and the broth recipe remains a family secret.

PHOTO CREDITS

p. 4: Row 1 (l–r): Anna Museaum; Courtesy of Gibson's Donuts; Ashlee Burlie; Courtesy of Fonuts

p. 4: Row 2 (l–r): Courtesy of Holtman's Donuts; Courtesy of Sublime Doughnuts; Courtesy of Glazed Donuts & Coffee; Courtesy of Federal Donuts

p. 4: Row 3 (l–r): Courtesy of the Holy Donut; Courtesy of Gibson's Donuts; Courtesy of Brenda's French Soul Food; Courtesy of Guru Donuts

p. 4: Row 4 (l–r): Union Square Donuts; Courtesy of Dutch Monkey Doughnuts; Courtesy of Blue Star Donuts; Courtesy of Congdon's Doughnuts: Family Restaurant & Bakery

p. 4: Row 5 (l–r): Courtesy of Dutch Monkey Doughnuts; Courtesy of La Salle Bakery; Courtesy of Cafe du Monde; Courtesy of Glazed Donuts & Coffee

p. 22–23: Courtesy of Congdon's Doughnuts: Family Restaurant & Bakery

p. 27–28: Courtesy of the Holy Donut

p. 43: Union Square Donuts

p. 48: Chelsea Kyle

p. 52: Courtesy of Flour Bakery

p. 67: Anna Museaum

p. 73: Dan Wang

p. 79: Todd Fuller

p. 85: Courtesy of Federal Donuts

p. 89: Courtesy of Fractured Prune

p. 93: Scott Suchman

p. 101: Farmers Fishers Bakers

p. 105: Sugar Shack Donuts

p. 109–110: Courtesy of Glazed Gourmet Doughnuts

p. 111–112: Courtesy of Dutch Monkey Doughnuts

p. 115: Courtesy of Sublime Doughnuts

p. 119–120: Courtesy of Glazed Donuts & Coffee

p 124: Courtesy of Rhino Doughnuts

p. 131–132: Courtesy of Cafe du Monde

p. 143: Courtesy of Holtman's Donuts

p. 152: Courtesy of Zingerman's Roadhouse

p. 163: Courtesy of Glam Doll Donuts

p. 164: Courtesy of Lindstrom Bakery

p. 167–169: Ashlee Burlie

p. 172–173: Courtesy of Hypnotic Donuts & Biscuits

p. 177–178: Courtesy of Peña's Donut Heaven & Grill

p. 185–186: Courtesy of Glazed & Confuzed Donuts

p. 199: Courtesy of Guru Donuts

p. 204–205: Courtesy of Sidecar Donuts

p. 211: Courtesy of Fonuts

p. 220: Courtesy of Brenda's French Soul Food

p. 225: Courtesy of Blue Star Donuts

p. 228: Courtesy of Voodoo Doughnuts

p. 239: Courtesy of Leonard's Bakery

Back cover:

Top right: Courtesy of Gibson's Donuts

Bottom right: Courtesy of Federal Donuts

GENERAL INDEX

An index of donut shops by state follows the general index

DONUT SHOPS AND RESTAURANTS BY STATE

WASHINGTON, DC

WYOMING

Rock Springs